I Ran Out of My Klompen:
A Personal History

W.W.II Holland to U.S. 1937-1955
by
Auké "Sy" Byle

BYLE PRESS
Oakland, Oregon
©2010

ON THE COVER:
Painting by artist, Julie Campbell, commissioned by the author in 1993.
A compilation of two family photos – one of Auké with the chickens,
and one of the Byle family's Snellveld home with goat.
Used with permission.

Compiled and Designed By:
Catherine Byle

Did is toegedaan aan myn vriend Willem v/d Dungen
Sept 21, 1936 - Dec 23, 2011

Willem   Auke

This printing is dedicated to the memory of my friend Willem v/d Dungen.

Our life long friendship started in the summer of 1943, playing in the 6 foot culvert near Willem's home. The culvert ran under the SteenWeg, with 12 to 18 inches of water in it. Our very own swimming hole stocked with minnows, frogs and lizards etc, and no mud, very classy!!

Willem and I are holding Willem's willow peeling tool, mentioned on page 18 of this book. The picture was taken when I was there for Willem's 75th birthday.

Willem loved, served and honored God with his life. He cared lovingly for his family, and always was there for his many friends. I am honored to be one of them!

He was a caring, meticulous gardener who loved and cared for his fruit trees as well as those of others. He had an incredible first hand knowledge of fruit trees and their care.

My very best friend, may you rest in peace, in Jesus Christ.

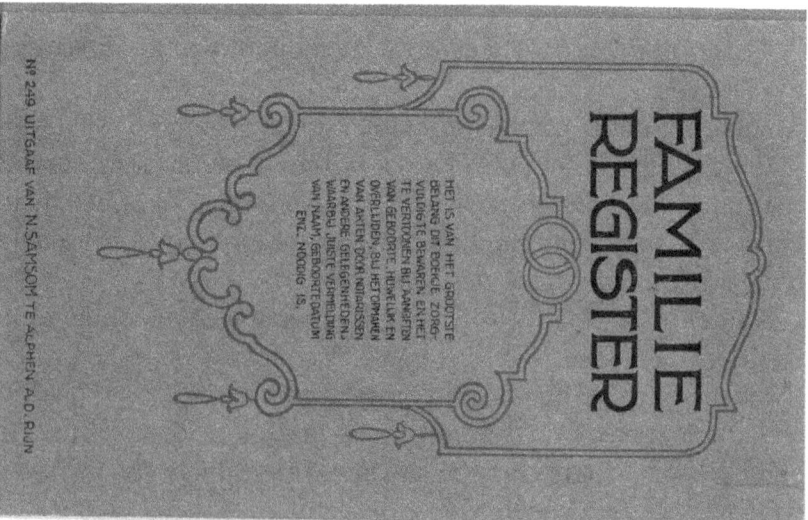

Wedding Book
Sybe Byl
and
Baukje
Franckena

2

Te KOUDUM, gemeente HEMELUMER

19 Mei — 1928 het huwelijk

Sijbe

geboren te *Deenum*,

zoon van *Piebe Bijl*,

en van *Geelje van der Hoek*,—

Bauke

geboren te *Molkwerum*,

dochter van *Auke Frankena*,

en van *Geltland Nolkkma*.—

3

OLDEPHAERT EN NOORDWOLDE, is op

voltrokken tusschen:

Bijl

den *29 Mei* — 190Y.

EN

Frankena,

den 15 *Januari* — 1906,

Vrij van zegel ingevolge art. 32, 6°., der Zegelwet 1917, juncto art. 136 Burgerlijk Wetboek.

De Ambtenaar van den burgerlijken stand,

Marriage
19 May 1928

KINDEREN UIT DIT HUWELIJK GEBOREN.

	VOORNAMEN.	GEBOREN		OVERLEDEN	
		TE	DEN	TE	DEN
1	*Rieka*	*gevisiterp*	*4 Aug. 1929*		
2	*Dettana*	*Wanrberg*	*12 Juny 1931*		
3	*Sieke Nisbaun*	*Wanrberg*	*20 Febr. 1937*		
4	*Geesje Gezina*	*Wanrberg*	*13 Febr. 1933*		
5	*Gerrit*	*Wanrberg*	*02 November 1946*		
6					
7					
8					
9					
10					
11					
12					

They had five children

Table of Contents

Introduction

A history of the early, exciting, tumultuous years of my life, my childhood, by Auké Siebren Byle, written especially for my boys - David, Darryl, Douglas, and Darrin – and those who care about me. I thank my wife, Ingrid, for always encouraging me, and Cathy (my son Doug's wife) for doing the hard work of putting my scribblings in order.

Ah, how time flies / And we fly along with it / Good we can know the flight Director.

--Auké "Sy" Byle, ©2009

Dedication

In memory of my late brothers, two terrific men of God. Pieter, though he was eight years my elder, never laid a hand on me or my sisters in anger. He had a great sense of humor which made him fun to be around. He loved and knew God's Word. Gerrit had the ability to make work fun – a walking, talking comedian. He had a freedom of manner that came from his confidence in God. Thanks for the many good times, "Bro."

Family History

Providence of the Netherlands, Friesland

Grandfather   Pieter Byl; b. February 29, 1872; d. December 28, 1930, of Spanish flu; Dairyman

Grandmother   Geertje Vander Hoek; b. August 31, 1871; d. May, 1969; Homemaker; very loving and kind to me; very good with animals; had 6 children.

1. Sjoek; b. March 27, 1899; d. 1991; Midwife
2. Tryntje; b. July 11, 1900; d. 1939, of Cancer; Homemaker
3. Sybé #1; d. at 6 months of age
4. Sybé; b. May 24, 1904; d. August 5th, 1973; Farmhand and Dairyman

5. Harm; b. July 1, 1907; d. 1941; Evangelist
6. Romke; b. September 28, 1909; d. 1977; Reformed Church Pastor; received a medal from the Queen for his work translating the Psalms into Friesian.

Grandfather   Auke Gerrit Franckena; b. 1868; d. 1938 of Tuberculosis; Cheese Factory-worker; played violin well, often for entertainment at the local Kroeg-bar.

Grandmother   Gelland Dokkum; b. October 17, 1876; d. March 1960, of a stroke following a minor surgery; had 4 children.

1. Grietje; b. December 14, 1904; d. 1990
2. Baukje; b. December 15, 1906; d. August 10, 1983, due to car accident
3. Twin boy and girl; Boy, death at age 7 days; Girl, Gerritje, died of Tuberculosis in her thirties.

In those days, when someone contracted T.B., the family put up a small, round building with lots of windows, which could be turned to follow the sun. Thus, a patient could lay in the sun all day and remain in isolation. Gerritje got scared, being there all alone, as the neighborhood boys would come and peek in the windows at night. So kind-hearted Auké (her dad) slept on the floor next to her bed, against the doctor's advice. That is how Auké contracted T.B. and died.

Friesland, Gelderland, and United States

Father   Sybé Byle started his first full-time job as a farm hand at age eleven.

Mother   Baukje Franckena's first paid job was picking up sheep manure for the gardens (no gloves).

Sybé and Baukje met when working for the same well-to-do farmer. Sybé held a position as a very promising all-around dairyman. Baukje was the head housekeeper, with a number of maids under her charge. Sybé and Baukje married on May 19, 1928, in Molkwerum, Baukje's hometown. Sybé did not miss a milking, even on his wedding day! They had 5 children.

1. Pieter; b. August 21, 1929; d. October 13, 2002; Michigan, United States
2. Gelland; b. June 13, 1931; lives in Washington, United States
3. Auké Siebren; b. April 2, 1937; lives in Oregon, United States
4. Geertje-Tryntje; b. February 13, 1943; lives in Washington, United States
5. Gerrit; b. November 22, 1946; d. March, 29, 2010; Wisconsin, United States

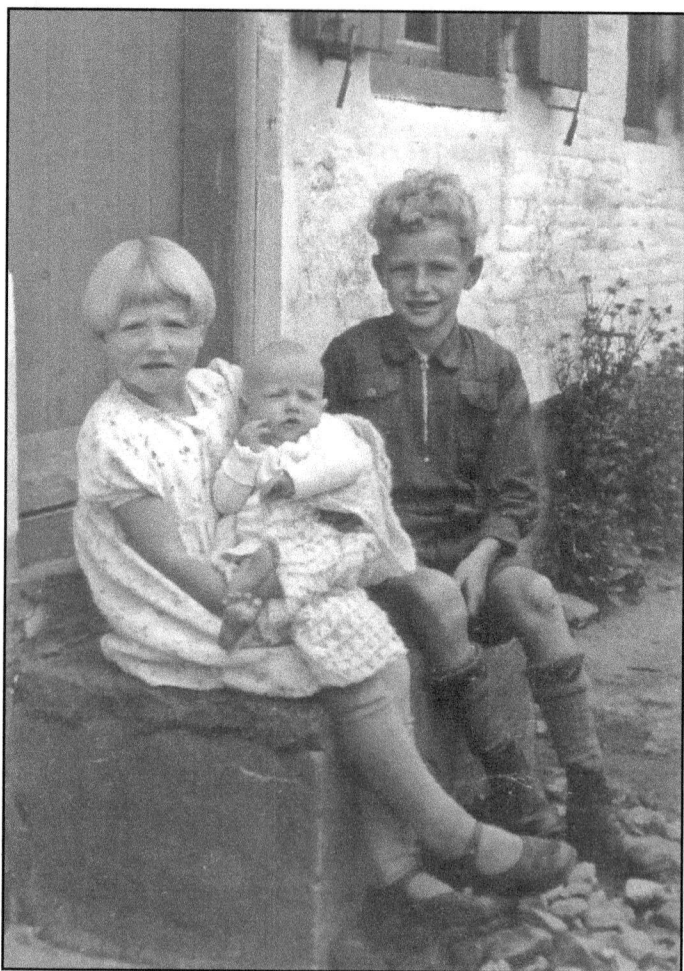

Pieter and Gelland with newborn Auké, 1937.

Snelleveld

A day of great relief for my mother, the 2nd of April (a Friday), 1937, I made my debut into the world of Baukje and Sybé Byle, joining my brother Pieter and sister Gelland in a little thatched-roof house. A happy, solid, hard-working family, well-able to adjust to the many challenges that lay ahead, Baukje and Sybé were Bible-believing Christians who looked to the God of Abraham, Isaac, and Israel as their life-compass.

Baukje, my mother, was soon challenged by my frequent, inconsolable crying as an infant. She wrote to my Tante Sjoek in Friesland that I cried a lot, wasn't gaining weight and that the doctor had no idea why. Tante Sjoek, who was a midwife and very knowledgeable about herbs, rode her bicycle all the way from Friesland to Gelderland (over 100 Kilometers) to check me out. She determined that I was allergic to cow's milk. She advised my mother to get a goat and feed me goat's milk. That worked! Tante Sjoek was right – even to this day I am mildly allergic to cow's milk.

The thatched roof of our house was made from reeds that grew in the marsh. We had no telephone or electricity. For water, we had a small hand pump in the rear of the house. One wall separated the front of the house containing kitchen, parlor and bedroom, from the rear of the house containing the pump and root cellar. A door in the middle of the wall provided passage between the two. The house had dirt for a floor in back and a wood floor in front. An outhouse served for a bathroom. We kids slept in the attic where we could hear the birds nesting in the roof. We could see, smell, and touch the reeds of the thatch. It felt very warm and secure.

The most memorable day at this house for me was May 10, 1940. I stood, looking out of the front window at big black planes, flying very low in the sky. A thundering noise filled my ears and I felt the house shaking. Mesmerized, I wet my pants in terror. Mem (my mom) came running in to the house, grabbed me, and ran out to the root cellar with me under her arm. My fears were partly allayed when she ran past the water pump

School Picture, 1942. Pieter, Auke, and Gelland Byl. Caption translation, "Out our school time."

without stopping, as the punishment for wetting my pants was to pump cold water on my bare little bottom. Mem climbed down into the root cellar, sat on a board, and placed me on her lap, wet pants and all. I asked, "What about Piet and Gellie and Heit (my dad)? Are the planes going to get them?!" Mem assured me, "Jesus will protect them." Then she put her arms around me and sang, "Fairest Lord Jesus, ruler of all nations,..." A calmness came over me, shutting out all the noise and terror of the planes! Indeed, Jesus did protect us all through the war and preserved us alive even when many around us did not survive.

I remember the day Piet and Gellie took me to school with them in Neerynen to have our picture taken. That was a big event for me, since I was not yet old enough for school. Gellie took me under her protection all day. We carried our lunch to school, as Pieter and Gellie did everyday. Lunch consisted of wheat bread with butter and sugar on it, and a small bottle of milk to drink, which we placed close to the wood stove so that it would stay warm until lunch time. Boy, was that good!

The area called Snelleveld, where we lived, was strictly country. Today, I am surprised that it even had a name. There

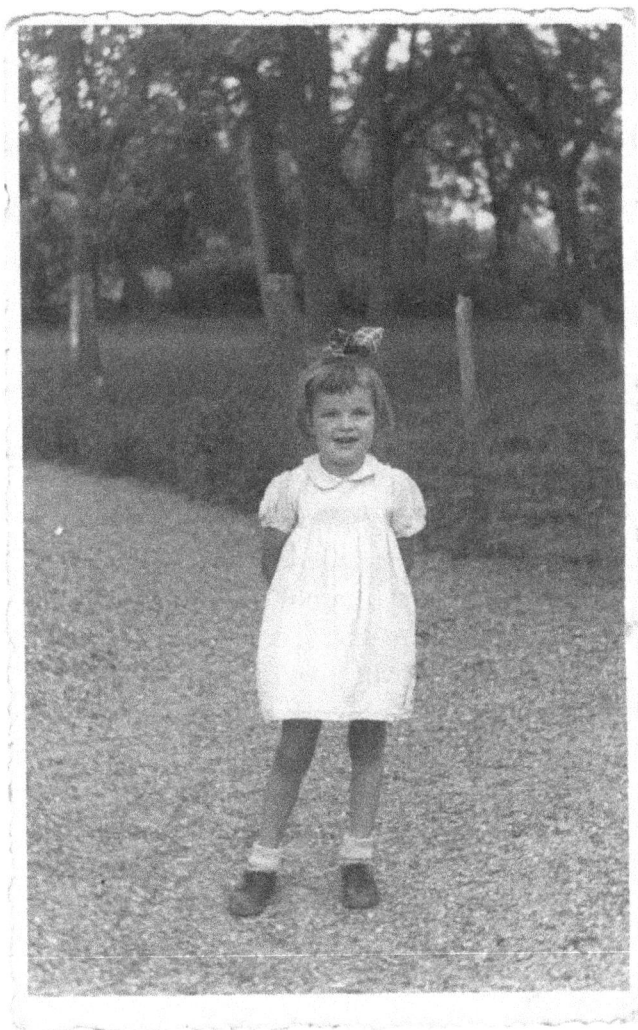

Neighbor girl, Anie

was only one other child my age in our neighborhood, a girl, called Anie. We played together, pretending to be farmers. We would pull up grass and make hay stacks, or pretend it was wheat and tie it into shocks. It was also my job to feed grass to our family's rabbits. That little chore made me appreciate my play time even more. Neither Anie or I had any toys that I recall. During those times, people generally did not have money for toys. But that did not stop us from having fun.

The pasture next to our house had sheep in it. I used to pick the wool left by the sheep on the barbed wire fence and give it to Mem. One day, a lady was visiting us who was interested in the wool and said she'd "love to have some!" So, at my industrious age of four years old, I recruited Anie to help, and we gathered wool for the visitor. I made a number of trips to the house with bags of wool. The lady was impressed and promised she would send me and Anie a package from where she lived in the big city of Utrecht. For weeks, I looked for that package, but it never came. After that, I figured city people were not honest. No one had ever lied to me like that before.

Mem had a green thumb. She could get plants to grow that others could not. As her trusted assistant, I learned how she would clean the rotten wood from the willow trees, put it in buckets, then mix the mulch with the soil. I remember our house was surrounded with plants – geranium, calendula, nasturtiums, hollihocks, and more.

Another memorable event that I recall from that neighborhood involved a dairy farmer who lived two houses down the road from ours. He would pass by our house everyday on his way out to milk his cows in the field. He would drive a small cart pulled by a big dog. The farmer usually sat on the cart, along with a couple milk cans and milk strainers. One day, the farmer himself was pulling the cart. Mem was so happy, she got the Dutch red-white-and-blue flag (strictly forbidden by the Nazis) and hung it up outside. Apparently, Mem had not approved of the farmer's treatment of the dog!

We lived about three miles from the farm my dad managed. So Heit had to pedal his bicycle to the farm twice a day, seven days a week. I remember during a snow storm he had to carry his bicycle. I felt so sorry for him when he returned home and came in through the back door, all cold and wet. Mem used to say that Heit did not have a humped back when they came from Friesland. She figured he got it pedaling the bicycle in bad weather. We had no rain gear back then.

I remember Mem taking me to the doctor in Waardenburg because I had a severe sore throat. The doctor informed her that the reason for my sore throat was that I had a third tonsil! Arrangements were made to have the tonsil removed. On the big day, Heit took me on the bicycle to the city of Tiel, fifteen or twenty miles away. I remember entering the Ziekenhuis (hospital). I walked into a room with several people in it. A nurse took my hand and set me on her lap. After fastening a rubber apron on me, they put a catch basin of some kind under my chin and stuffed something in my mouth so that I couldn't close it. The doctor held a couple of metal devices over a small blue flame next to him, then stuck them in my mouth. After working the devices in my mouth a little, he pulled them out, and the nurse pushed me forward as I bled from my mouth into the basin.

The bleeding stopped rather soon, and the nurse told me I had been "a brave young man." The nurse stayed with me and took me to a room where my dad was waiting for me. He took me to Oom Driek's drug store, where they put me on a couch and covered me up so I could rest. Heit then went away, to my distress, but when he returned he came with a present for me because I had not cried. The present was two little wooden horses on wheels pulling a wagon. I was so excited! That is the most memorable

Heit with horses, circa 1930.

present I ever got while we lived in Holland. We would get simple, practical gifts, like new socks or something else handmade, on St. Nick's Day December 5th. But this gift was store-bought and a very special surprise, as my parents did not have money to buy toys. Heit bundled me up and took me home that same afternoon on the bicycle, another fifteen to twenty miles.

At home, I got the royal treatment. I got to sleep in the bed-stee downstairs. Heit fixed a board across my lap so I could run my horses and wagon across it. I had to stay in bed for about two days, which was not to my liking. I do not recall feeling a bit of pain!

I remember baby Geertje's baptism. A most beautiful black coach, drawn by a black horse came to pick us up and take us to the church in Geldermalsen. The coachman had on a black top hat, a whip sat on his left side, and he wore the whole attire befitting a proper coachman. Piet and Heit got to sit on the outside with the coachman. I had to sit inside. The inside had two seats. I remember looking at the door and handle and the view through the window. It was a nice day out, but I was stuck inside. Tante Sjoek was there, too – being a midwife, I suppose that was a good thing – having ridden her bicycle again all the way from Friesland. The trip from our house to Geldermalsen was about ten kilometers. The coach waited for us during the service and, after church, took us for coffee and gebak (goodies), then back home. I don't remember any of the church service, just the coach ride to and from and the coffee time.

By the time I was five years old, Heit would sometimes take me with him to the farm where he worked. The farm that my dad managed belonged to a Gentleman-farmer (in other words, someone who enjoys owning a farm, but has someone else do the work). Heit had taken over management of the farm at the death of his father in 1930 of Spanish Flu. The owner's home was traditional with home in the front and barn in the back half of the building. The cows were kept in the barn half during the Winter, with hay stored in a loft above them. Pigs and calves were kept in a building behind the barn, with nice brick pavers for walking in between. Another barn to the left of the cow barn and house

Farm that Heit managed. Modern photo, by Sy Byle.

was for the horses and wagon. I liked being in the barn in the Winter. It was nice and warm, and there were always friendly cats to play with in the hay. Heit would spend considerable time feeding and brushing the horses. Heit let me walk under them, telling me to be sure to talk to them, so as not to spook them. I can still remember the way the horses smelled and the way they would lift their heads out of the manger to look at me, as if saying, "Hi, little boy." They were very tame. I learned all their names, because Heit always talked to them and called them each by name. Even when Heit was working them in the field, the horses would respond to me. They would look at me if I called out to them by name, and it seemed to me that they smiled.

The Knotwilgen (Knot Willows), were cut back every fall after the leaves were off. Farmers and workers would bundle the pruned twigs according to diameter size then store the bundles in a ditch of two to three feet of water. In the spring, they would hold a peeling-work bee. We kids got to work the narrower (¼ inch to ½ inch) twigs. Each branch was around five feet long. Peeling the willow branches was a job I really enjoyed, and our neighbor, Hannes Blom, told me I was very good at it. One

Knotwilgen (Knot willows) in Winter. Modern photo by Gijsje van der Heijden.

peeled the twigs by hitting them into a metal y-shaped, spring-loaded device, then pulling them through. The bark peeled right off, neatly and cleanly. The grown men pulled the thicker branches (½ inch – 2 inches), which were used to make heavy-duty mats. The narrow twigs were used for weaving baskets and other crafts. My sister, Gellie, and her friend Huipie De Waal could weave baskets. All I can remember doing as a five-year-old was weaving mats, which took some time, as I had to work the ends in neatly, beginning and ending. As straight as mat-weaving was, it was a challenge for me to learn at that age.

The heavy willow mats were used as a way of life by the farmers to cross the many drainage ditches, sometimes six feet, sometimes twelve feet wide, that surrounded the fields. They would place heavy beams across a ditch, then lay the willow mats on top. They could then drive their teams and equipment across. To illustrate, there was a famous local story of two brothers working in a field outside Waardenburg. One had been plowing, the other came behind with a tooth harrow. When the one plowing got done, in order to expedite the move to the next field, he took up the mats and beams and went to the next field, leaving his brother stranded. Before they could rectify the error, a neighbor went by with his team and took note. He gleefully broadcast the story, and the two brothers never lived it down. In our "fruit belt" (Betuwe) of Holland, just about all the containers were woven willow baskets. These were used especially at Cherry harvest time. I was not big enough to pick the cherries (boy, were they sweet!), so my job was to chase starlings. I was given a large wooden rattle on a four-foot-long pole. I had to walk up and down the orchard, keep a sharp look out for starlings and turn the rattle at any that I saw. Occassionally, I did use the rattle to pull some cherries with my reach. Mr. Sterenberg, for whom I worked, did not appreciate it!

In 1943, Heit and Mem finally found a house they could buy, located much closer to Heit's work (about ½ a kilometer). We would move into civilization right next to a dike and a dual train track. Between our house and the dike were a wide drainage ditch and a small orchard. The ditch was a great place for fishing with bobber and worms, and for duck egg-hunting in the spring. About one-and-a-half kilometers away was the Waal River, a very large, important waterway for freight boats

Cherry Picking crew, 1954.
Willem Van Den Dungen, back row, second from the left.

Hoenderick (Willow basket) and rachet for cherry picking, property of Willem Van Den Dungen. Modern photo by Gijsje van der Heijden, 2010.

Knotwilgen in Spring. Modern photo by Gijsje van der Heijden.

Waardenburg

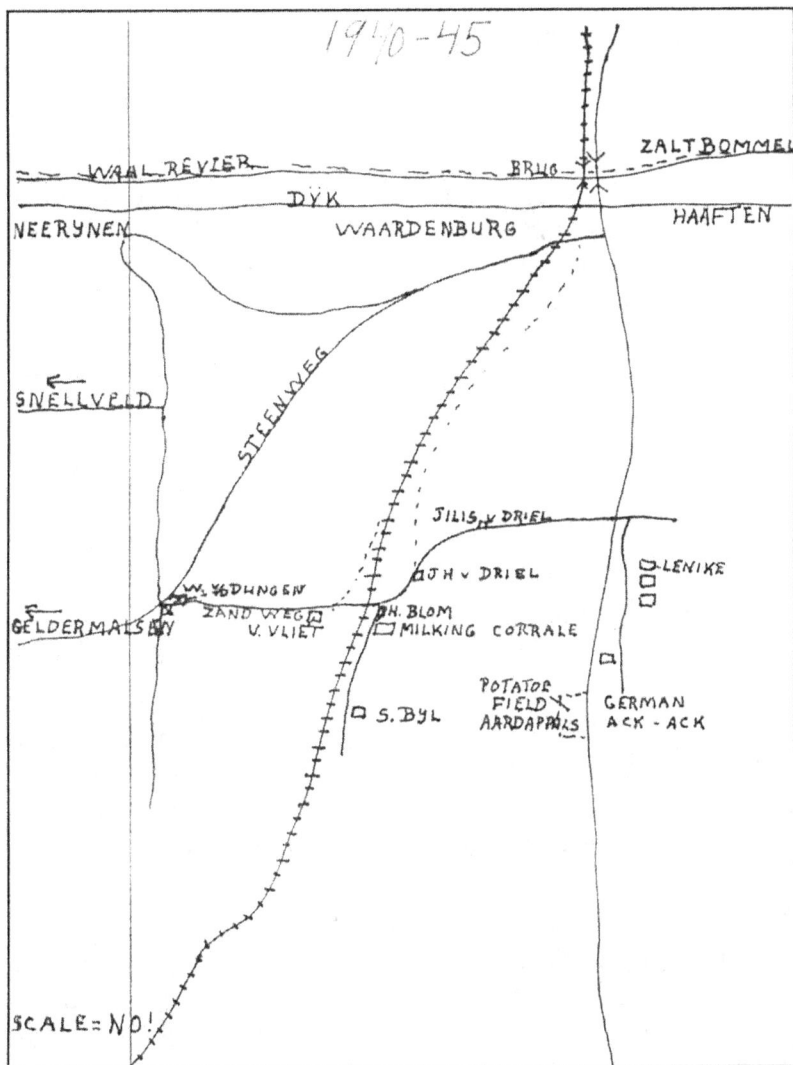

1940-45

WAAL REVIER — BRUG — ZALTBOMMEL

DYK

NEERYNEN — WAARDENBURG — HAAFTEN

SNELLVELD

STEENWEG

JILIS v DRIEL

JH v DRIEL — LENIKE

W. v DUNGEN
ZAND WEG
GELDERMALSEN — V. VLIET — H. BLOM
MILKING CORRALE

S. BYL — POTATOE FIELD
AARDAPPELS — GERMAN ACK-ACK

SCALE = NO!

Map by Sy Byle, 2010.

going to and from Germany. The bridge that crossed the Waal had two lanes for automobiles plus two lanes for bicycles and pedestrians. A double-track train bridge crossed the river just on the east side of the automobile bridge. Our new house sat on the Paralelweg (the road to the house was parallel to the railroad) near Waardenburg.

I spent a lot of time watching the self-propelled river barges, and neat tugs pulling and pushing barges and work boats. As I watched the boats and trains, I tried to decide whether I wanted to be a tug boat captain or a train engineer. I leaned toward becoming a steam locomotive engineer. But as the war progressed, I saw trains get strafed by fighter planes, people screaming and jumping out while the train was still running. That dampened my enthusiasm!

During the first couple of years of the war, things had been rather peaceful for us. But after the allied landing in Normandy in 1944, we saw a lot more fighter and dive-bomber action, as the allies then had bases in Europe proper, rather than having to fly across the English Channel to refuel. The fighter planes and dive bombers provided me with a lot of, what I figured to be, safe entertainment. On the other side of our potato field, German anti-aircraft artillery guarded the Waal bridges. Every now and then, when the fighter planes would strafe the artillery, if we were out in the field, we would dive into the nearest ditch. The fighters would open up and it would rain empty shell casings and connecting rings. Once the shooting was over, I would round up the casings and rings, in between digging potatoes.

During the attack, the Germans would shoot at the incoming planes with machine guns and with bigger 88mm anti-aircraft guns when the fighters pulled away. It sounded like thunder and the ground would shake. But we felt safe, as the fighter planes were very accurate, within yards of their target (unlike the bombers who could be miles off-target, a reality which we experienced very close to home – more on that later). The Germans would shoot over us. We were much safer than people two to three kilometers away, where the bullets would come down.

P-51 Fighter taunts the German 88mm Ack-Ack as Auke looks on from Paralel weg.
Darryl Byle drew this especially for this book! (©2014). Used by permission.

I really enjoyed watching the planes. One day, I saw an unusual sight as a fighter plane (a P-51) flew fairly high. The big artillery started to shoot at him. You could see the puffs of smoke as the shells exploded. The fighter started to circle around and around, and when the shells got close, he would tip his wing. After playing around for some time like this, the fighter flew right through the middle of the exploding shells, rolled twice, then tipped his wing and flew west. I figured that when this pilot tipped his wings, he was saying, "Close, but no cigar!" I understand now that there were a lot of eighteen- to twenty-year-old fighter pilots. I figure this pilot was probably one of them. He probably had a good laugh, but his cockiness might have gotten him shot down – the Germans were not playing.

At this house, we had more land. There was a neat mixed orchard of pears, apples and plums between the house and the dike. I recall helping Mem put baby Geertje's play pen under the big blue plum tree. Somehow, at one or two years old, Geertje got her hands on a nice juicy plum, and by the time Mem saw her, Geertje had downed the pit. Mem immediately ran to get her bicycle and put Geertje in the baby seat on the back, preparing to ride to the doctor. Mem instructed me to go to Driek Blom's, our next door neighbor. Mem proceeded as fast as she could pedal to the doctor's office in Waardenburg. The doctor told her to relax, that the pit would go the natural route without any negative effects. Sure enough, it did.

At the end of the orchard was about five acres of woods, with the ever-present drainage ditch. Heit built a bomb shelter at the edge of the woods, about three hundred feet behind the house – a hole (4 feet wide by 7 feet long, by 4 feet deep) in the ground lined with straw; rail ties topped with three to four feet of sod formed the roof. We entered through a door in the side of the shelter. This was a farmer's answer to the big cement bomb shelters. In reality, it served only as a fragment and bullet shelter. Any direct hit by a bomb would have blown us to bits and pieces, a fact of which we lived very much aware.

Mem, my younger sister Geertje, my dog and I did spend a lot of time in that shelter. My dog, a small, yellow terrier mix, would sit curled up in my lap. I recall one particular time, when we and our neighbor Driek sat in there during one of the dreaded "carpet bombing" raids. The bombs were falling, and the heavy artillery and machine guns were firing, making a deafening amount of noise. Whenever a bomb fell close by, the ground would shake, and dirt would fall on us all. Mem sat calmly with Geertje on her lap, singing Christian songs. I distinctly remember that Mrs. Blom did not sing, but instead, would scream at the top of her lungs, much to my disgust. I wanted to yell at her, "Just sing along with my mother!!" It made me respect Mem.

Byl family, 1943. Sybé, Baukje holding Geertje, Pieter, Auké, Gelland.

Due to Heit's work, Mem was the family spiritual leader by default. She would pray before every meal – not just, "God bless this food," – naming names, places, events, etcetera that were on her heart. Then, when we were done eating, she would read a whole chapter in the Bible, followed by a prayer of thanksgiving. Scriptures like Matthew Chapter Five, in which Jesus teaches, "love your enemies, bless those who curse you, do good to those who hate you; and pray for those who spitefully use you and persecute you, that you may be sons of your Father in heaven; for He makes His sun rise on the evil and on the good, and sends rain on the just and on the unjust," prepared us for the hardship of war. This gave us all direction and a realization that God was always there. We came to understand that God was sustaining us, even through very trying times.

We started going to the Christian Reformed church in Zaltbommel, as it was closer now than our former church, Geldermalsen Christian Reformed. The best feature of going to church for me became crossing the Waal. It was, and still is, a busy, exciting river. Another was being fed peppermints during the service to pacify me. But I don't recall too much else of church other than that I felt bored from sitting so long. My faith came mainly from watching my parents in action.

Both of my parents were very comfortable talking about their faith. I recall once listening to Heit talking at the dinner table about a funeral for Cris Sannen's dad, a local grocery store owner. At the service, the priest had said Sannen had "earned the right to speak to God face to face." All thought the Sannens were great people – very honest. Cris would deliver groceries door-to-door with horse and coach. Even though they were Catholic, they were much respected by the protestant town majority. My folks were also very fond of them and believed them to be true Christians. Heit agreed Sannen was a good, honest man. But he argued that he still needed Jesus, as everyone did, as his go-between to God. The way my father explained it I was able to make sense of it, even at seven years of age.

Another feature of our Waardenburg home was a nearby

pond. It inspired me to take up poaching for duck eggs. Usually, I went alone, as Pieter had to work. There were some dangers attached to my duck egg hunting. For one, I could get caught by the hunting supervisor, Vander Elst, who patrolled all of Baroness Mevrouw van Paland's lands. Secondly, since the task required me to wade into the pond, sometimes chest-deep, there was a risk of drowning. But I was used to playing in the water, rocking my row boat on the pond, etcetera, and was confident in my dog-paddling skills. I hunted eggs in both the pond near our house and the drainage ditch along the Paralel Weg. In spite of the risks, my parents did not stop me.

I loved duck-egg-hunting, and thought that I was pretty good at it! The procedure was simple. Before the hunt, I would keep an eye out during the day to see where the ducks were hanging out. A male duck alone would indicate the presence of a female setting on a nest nearby. I started by getting up early in the morning and walking along the water's edge, beating the marshy growth with a stick. The setting duck would usually wait until I had got within ten feet or so, then fly off. I could easily locate the nest with the eggs. Then, I had to check which eggs were edible and which had baby ducks in them. To do this, I would lay an egg flat in the palm of my hand, then put my hand in the water, submerging the egg entirely. If the egg stood on end, it had the start of a duck in it, and I would put it back in the nest. If it stayed flat in my hand underwater, it was good to eat! I took home the edible ones and left the rest in the nest.

Once I had found a nest, I could return to the same nest every couple of days for a week or two, raiding the new eggs. But one had to be careful not to disturb the nest, because the ducks would not come back. The ducks usually kept from eight to twelve eggs in a nest. The most I ever got were nine good eggs out of one nest! On that occasion, I got soaking wet, as the nest was attached to some reeds and kind of floated. I did not float. I sank about chest deep in the marshy water, but it was worth it! Fortunately, Pieter happened to be with me that time. Since I had found the eggs, I got the credit, but Pieter had helped me.

The first place I saw a sign "Voor Jooden Verboden" (For

Jews Forbidden) was by a park in Zaltbommel on our way to the market. At the market, one always saw Jews. They were especially noticeable once they started wearing the yellow Star of David on their clothing. I recall once going to the market with my dad and watching a Jew demonstrate a peeling knife. It worked so slick that Dad bought one. But at home, neither he nor Mem could make it peel worth a darn.

One day, I was with Mem on our way to Zaltbommel, when the German guards stopped us. We showed them our permits and I.D., but the guards were still suspicious. They ordered me off of Mem's bicycle, took my stocking hat off, and ordered me to remove my wrap-around muffler. One of the guards went through my hair to see if I had dark roots. Then I knew what they were looking for – Jewish kids. I had very white-blond hair, and could be mistaken for being bleached. People who had hidden Jews bleached the hair of the children to help them escape to safety behind the allied lines. The Canadian troops at that time had been pushing the Germans back.

As crazy as it seems, even when the Nazis were losing the war, they were determined to kill as many Jews as possible. I remember a N.S.B. (Nationaal Socialistiche Beweging; trans. National Socialistic Movement) member who gave us school kids (grades 1st through 3rd) a lecture on what today we would call "policital correctness." He spoke about how bad the Jews were, and taught that everything wrong in our society was the fault of the Jews. The Nazis offered a big reward for turning in Jewish children. Many Jewish kids were hidden in attics or other small rooms, without neighbors or even family members in the same house knowing about it. This targeting of the Jews was a mystery to me as a child. For one thing, I couldn't understand why the reward for turning in a Jewish kid was bigger than the reward for an allied flyer. I admired the flyers and figured they must be a lot more valuable than little kids! When I came home from school, I told Mem how bad the Jews were. Mem looked hard at me, then said, "Jesus is a Jew (Jesus is een Jood)." That really helped me get a grip on the situation! That is all that Mem

Bomb shell fragment lodged in the door of our Waardenburg house,
September 17th, 1944. Photo by Ingrid Byle.

said, or could say, so that she could not later be accused of speaking in support of the Jews. Knowing Mem, I am sure she prayed her little boy would understand, and I did.

Mid-morning, on September 17th, 1944, I experienced the most terrifying bombing raid of my life, coinciding with the famous airborne raid on Arnhem - Operation Market Garden. As my family headed for the bomb shelter near our house, all I could see was a solid blue wall of flames and smoke coming toward us. Planes sped toward us (flying 100 to 140 miles per hour, I later learned as an adult). Bombs fell around us as we descended into the shelter. After the raid, we found aluminum propellers laying around, measuring about five to six inches long, that had somehow made the bombs explode before they hit the ground. We learned later that the operation had been an anti-personnel bombing raid with several other drop zones, all within forty kilometers of our place (2800 tons of high-explosive fragment bombs dropped that one day). I watched my brother Pieter dig a bomb fragment out of our front door! The fragment was one inch by five-eighths of an inch. If that fragment had instead hit a human body, what a huge hole it would have made!

A week later, I was playing at my friend Willem Van Den

Dungen's house, when I saw about a-hundred-and-twenty Canadian prisoners of war being marched down the road by a number of heavily-armed Germans. The Canadians marched rather well, I thought, in their good-looking uniforms, carrying full field packs and still wearing their helmets. They looked rather impressive. I was disappointed they had lost their fight with the Germans.

I have fond memories of working in the garden with Mem. She grew a vegetable garden year 'round. The produce depended on the season. Even in winter, we had crops like kale and brussel sprouts. We harvested carrots during every season. Gardening could have been a drag, but Mem made it fun. She would sing Christian songs. Geertje was close by in her cradle. My job was to weed the carrots and also to thin them – every time I see carrots in the garden, now, I think of Mem. As soon as I was done, I could go play along the drainage ditch, where I would usually find frogs and salamanders. That vegetable garden played an important role in our survival as hunger became rampant, especially in the cities, during the winter of 1944-45.

By this point in the war, the Germans had closed our school in order to use it for an ammunition dump, much to my delight! The allies usually avoided bombing churches and schools, so of course, the Germans took advantage of it. Since school had been closed, Heit and Mem sent me to a lady teacher's house in Waardenburg for lessons. One activity I remember doing for her was the "Aap-Noot-Mies" board. The board had seventeen different pictures on it, to teach the letters of the alphabet. My task was to find matching letters and place them under each picture on the board. When finished, my reward was getting to work her modern marvel – a gramophone! She would let me wind it up, then she would put the needle on the record! What a thrill! I had never seen anything like it before, and I got to wind it up! I bragged about it to my family and friends. I went twice a week for about an hour lesson. For payment, I brought the teacher a can of fresh milk.

Other than the teacher's gramophone, my exposure to

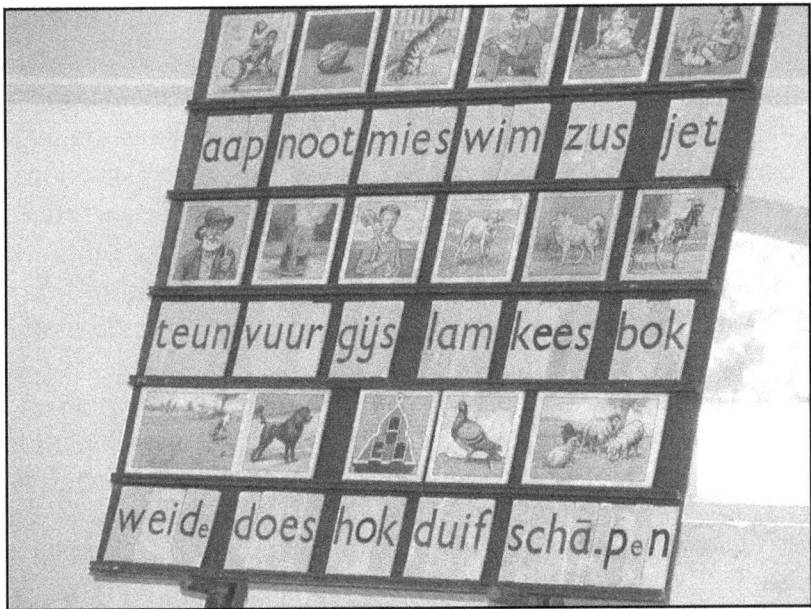

*Photo used with permission - http://commons.wikimedia.org/wiki/File:Aap_noot_
mies.jpg. (Accessed July 8, 2010.)*

music was limited, especially since radios were outlawed by
the Nazis. Our family did sing a lot. Mem would sing or hum
while going about her daily tasks, and that encouraged us to sing,
too, no matter what we were doing. Piet and Gellie both played
harmonica, as did a lot of folks. Piet was exceptionally good
at it. He could even play while pedaling his bicycle. Teenagers
like Piet and Gellie would parody old tunes, like "Roll Out the
Barrel," by making up lyrics that mocked the Germans and anyone
associated with them, such as the Dutch girls that dated them.
Those were considered street songs. Of course, we sang songs
at church, too – Christian hymns and choruses. Cris Sannen, our
local grocer, would play his piano for me in the evenings when
I delivered his milk, a job I started at age six. I enjoyed the
music although I often did not know the tune – I suppose he
played a lot of Classical pieces. Cris played in the Waardenburg
Band, which often performed on Friday or Saturday evenings.
The bandstand was on the West side of the railroad along the
Steenweg. Sometimes the Germans would play and sing at the

bandstand, too. Piet, Gellie and I would go listen. We had to sit or stand in the grass or along the Steenweg. Younger kids my age liked to play tag, but that was not appreciated by the older folks. I really liked the music, especially when the Germans sang! Of course, we had to be in by curfew, eight o'clock, no exceptions.

Food was a very precious commodity, controlled as much as possible by the powers that be. Gellie and I went into the wheat fields to glean wheat (just like Ruth in the fields of Boaz). The men harvested the wheat by cutting it with a sickle in one hand and a hook on a short stick in the other. Another worker would come behind, gathering handfuls and wrapping it around to make a bundle. Two other workers would follow, each putting bundles together in a shock (usually 10 bundles to a shock). Gleaners, like Gellie and I, could pick up whatever was left on the ground.

We took the gleaned wheat home, spread it out on a tarp in the back of the house, then flailed it. The flail was made of two heavy sticks, one long (about 4 feet) and one short (about 2 feet), tied together with a rope or leather strap. The long stick was for holding, the short one beat the wheat. One developed a knack and rhythm. I liked flailing the wheat and was pretty good at it for a seven-year-old. After flailing, we put the wheat in buckets and took it outside among the brush and reeds so no one would see us. There was always a chance of some government official confiscating it. Gellie and I would wait for a breeze, then, standing on a chair, carefully pour out the wheat into a tub. The breeze would blow the chaff away. We repeated this until all the chaff was gone. Mem would store the wheat in tin cans to use as needed. She would let me grind it in our small coffee grinder. I liked working with Gellie, because she was really good at whatever she did, and that made me look good, too.

Threshing time on the farm was fun for me. Heit's friend owned a threshing machine and tractor. He would let me sit on the tractor and help to bag the grain. I had to stay away from the belts of the threshing machine, but I got to watch while he oiled them and I saw that he held some kind of tube on the belts as they were turning. It was a fun thing for me to be around. My job was to hook an empty grain bag up to a grain shoot, then flip a lever over as soon as the bag was full. The lever would direct the flow of grain between two bags – Left for left-side bag, Right for right-side bag, Up for stop. Then the threshing-man would quickly tie the bag with a short string and set it on a platform. Heit drove one of three horse-and-wagons that hauled the sheaves of wheat from the field to the machine.

During threshing, a government inspector stayed on hand and counted the bags of grain. Around ten in the morning, the lady of the house came out and invited everyone inside for "real" coffee and goodies. Everyone came in, including the inspector. I got some cookies and boiled milk – it was great! When we all returned from our break, the inspector was very upset. Somebody had apparently removed some bags of wheat. The inspector had words with the threshing-man and the farmer, but he could not prove anything or implicate anyone, because the farmer, his workers and the neighbors had all been inside the house. That was one of the ways the farmers beat the system.

The socialistic government attempted to control every aspect of life. Farmers had to register all their animals. One could not butcher an animal without first getting government permission. If permission was granted, you had to report when the butchering would take place, so that a "controleur" (inspector) could supervise and stamp the approved meat. An inspector could drop in anytime to make sure all your food had a stamp on it. If a person was caught butchering his or her own meat without a permit, that person could be shot on sight.

Farmers took the risk of getting around the meat controls by butchering in secret. After the war, I asked Heit how we always seemed to have plenty of meat, because I had never witnessed a secret butchering take place, nor smelled the evidence of it later. Heit explained that Mem would take us kids away for three to four hours, probably visiting friends, while three neighbors came over to help. They would take the animal, usually a pig, into the woods to butcher it and quarter it to split among the four families. By doling out only a quarter, no one would have a lot of meat to hide at a time. Only old trusted neighbors were let in on the take. The donation of animal for slaughter was rotated among the four neighbors. Another way they would get around the laws involved bribing the inspector with a smoked ham or some other agreed-upon cut. In that case, a farmer would secure a permit to butcher one pig, but on the slaughter date, he would butcher two or three. The inspector would stamp all three. Then the farmer would distribute the meat among friends and arrange to deliver the ham to the inspector's house, so the inspector could never be implicated by taking it himself.

I remember one day that we kids played hide and seek, I sneaked into my parents' bedroom to hide. Our folks' room was strictly off-limits, so I figured no one would find me there. I opened the closet door and squeezed in between the clothes. I bumped into a hard object. It was a nice big smoked ham! I knew that no one was supposed to know about that ham. So I scurried out of there and hid under the living room sofa instead.

Heit ran a dairy which milked a herd of cows by hand. In the spring, summer and fall, he and other workers milked outdoors in a milking corral that was set up in the pasture. The milk cans would sit on the roadside of the corral fence. Two, large funnel-shaped strainers sat atop the cans. When a milker finished milking a cow, he would walk over to the fence and dump the milk out of a pail into the strainer, checking first, of course, to see that the can had plenty of room for the milk without the milk running over. A milker would sit on a one-legged wooden stool and hold the milk pail with his knees, the pail meanwhile resting either on the ground or on the milker's wooden shoes.

Wooden shoes, one of the marks of Dutch culture, had some great benefits for the dairyman. They were warm and water proof. In a milking corral, they stood up well to muddy conditions and the threat of getting stepped on by a cow! If a cow stood on your toes, it wouldn't hurt in a wooden shoe. But if you were wearing leather or rubber boots or shoes, it would hurt like the devil and could break your foot. Wooden shoes were widely popular and available. Every locality had its wooden shoe-maker. He would come around with his horse and wagon full of wooden shoes – plain ones, fancy painted ones and carved shoes. I had fun trying them on.

But, back to the milking. If a cow had a propensity to walk away or kick while being milked, each milker had a short rope with which to tie the back legs together quickly. Even with back legs tied, a cow might still hop if she was determined. If she did, the milker would also tie her head up. But most of the cows just stood, calmly chewing their cud. It made for a peaceful, pleasent setting.

The German army, of course, had to eat and drink, and they tried to acquire as much food as possible locally. Since they were the conquering army, they could demand and get it. They did have the consideration to pay for their supplies. However, they also printed the money. Towards the end of the war, there were no supplies in the store. "Niks in de winkel alles in de kelder," was a common saying – "Nothing in the store, everything in the basement." The farmers still produced, but the processing infrastructure no longer functioned. So the German army tapped the farmers directly.

Heit had to supply the army with two cans of milk twice a week. They dispatched a soldier with horse and wagon to pick up the milk. Our soldier's name was Hans. He was a private first class with the anti-aircraft artillery. The first time I met Hans, he stood holding his horse by the bridle and talking to it. I figured he must be an o.k. soldier if he talked to his horse. So I went over and talked to Hans. We spoke German, since my German was better than his Dutch – we had no problem communicating.

After our first meeting, I looked forward to Hans coming. I often sat on the seat of the wagon next to Hans, while he showed me a picture of his family. In the picture stood his boy, about my age, and Hans said we looked a lot alike. Then he would rub my hair and laugh. His vrouw (wife) and two daughters were also in the picture. Hans often repeated to me, "Wir haben den krieg nicht gewollt," ("We did not want this war!")

Sketch of Hans and Auké on wagon, by Kayla Byle (©2010).

One day, another soldier came in Hans' place. I asked him, "Waar is Hans." He ignored me. He did not want to speak to me. So I asked my dad, and he, too, avoided the question, which was unusual. Heit was usually very easy for me to talk to. When we got home that night I told Mem that Hans had not come, and that another soldier had come instead. Heit then told what had happened to Hans. He had received a message informing him that his wife and children had been killed in an allied bombing raid. Upon hearing the news, Hans committed suicide by shooting himself! It hurt me to think how awful Hans had felt about losing his family. I wrestled with my feelings, because I knew the allied planes, flying by the hundreds, were bombing Germany in order to free us. But I did not like the idea of those bombs killing people like Hans' family! I talked to Mem about it. She also felt sad that so many people had to die in the bombing raids.

One nice warm spring day, as I walked barefooted (which I did a lot) on my way to a field where Heit was plowing with four horses, two German soldiers in a field next to Heit's stopped me. They were stealing potatoes out of a field storage. Farmers would store potatoes in a wide trench about six feet wide by twenty-five feet long and about two feet deep. The farmer would line the trench with straw, put the potatoes in then cover the potatoes with straw and about one foot of soil on top. The soldiers motioned for me to come help them by holding the bag, but I walked on. Then one of the men yelled, picked up his rifle and aimed it at me. That got my attention! I went over to them and held the bag. They filled several bags full until Heit stopped his team across from us and motioned for me to come to him. The German soldier gave me two cigarettes for my dad and told me I could go. Whew! I thanked him and ran to Heit. Soon after I left, the farmer whose potatoes they were stealing arrived on his bicycle. He told them in very colorful Dutch to get the hell out of there. One soldier picked up his rifle and aimed it at the farmer. The farmer jumped on his bicycle and told them he would turn their stealing hides in to their commandant. As he pedaled away,

Jacobus Van Den Dungen,
d. Nov. 8, 1944

the German shot into the railroad dike. The farmer yelled back that the soldier could go shoot the devil – "Jouw rot mof!" (You rotten German!) I was impressed with the gutsy farmer.

Early one morning, in the Fall of 1944, Jacobus Van Den Dungen ("Cobus") and Hannes Blom walked by our house on the Paralelweg, en route to a beet field close by our place. They carried beet spades – a very handy tool, easy to use. Their job that day was to harvest sugar beets by digging them up and throwing them into piles, to be picked up later with horse and wagon. Jacobus waved to me, because I was friends with his younger brother, Willem. I waved back. That afternoon, as so often happened by this point in the war, the allied fighters and dive-bombers flew over, shooting up whatever was on their list of targets. My family and I ran to our bomb shelter. Meanwhile, Hannes dove into the ditch that ran alongside the beet field. Hannes called to Cobus, who sat in the field rolling a cigarette, to urge him to get in the ditch. Cobus answered, "Soon as I get my cigarette rolled!" The next time that Hannes looked, Cobus was laying flat on the ground, a large bullet hole in his neck. As soon as the shooting stopped, Hannes ran home past our house shouting, "Cobus is dood! Cobus is dood!" (Cobus is dead!)

Soon a whole lot of people came to the beet field, making a lot of noise. Mem, holding Geertje, stood with Gellie and I, watching as the crowd passed on the trail about ten feet from our house. A little later, they passed by our house again, carrying Jacobus on a ladder covered with blankets. His parents followed right behind the ladder. I remember watching his mother, crying, "Myn Jonge, myn Jonge, Cobus," (My boy, my boy, Cobus) over and over. The weight of the family's sadness moved me. It hadn't been that long since Cobus and I had waved to each other so happily. Years later, when my friend Willem grew up, he named his son, Jacobus, in memory of his brother.

Hunger brought people out from the city to beg and trade for food. People came in droves, down the roads, pushing and pulling carts and wheelbarrows, etcetera, loaded with items to trade for food. They had clocks, clothes, furniture, brooms, whatever they could bring. I remember Mem trading for a broom once. We were only small farmers and had very little, if any, surplus. But Mem did feed them, and let them sleep in the hay in the barn, when it became too close to curfew for them to go home. Most came from large cities, like Utrecht, at least thirty-five kilometers away. At curfew, everyone had to be off the road and inside houses, or you could be shot on the spot. The S.S. patrols were especially feared as they were much quicker to shoot than the regular army.

Having guests in the barn sometimes posed a problem, because guys would smoke cigarettes while lying in the hay. Of course, Heit would ask them not to. I remember one time a woman guest came to the house to inform Heit about a man who was smoking in the hay. Heit told the man to leave. The man was, of course, terrified of the German patrols. He wound up sleeping in front of the cows.

On one occasion we traded for a two-wheeled cart. Heit helped me make a harness for my billy goat out of old threshing machine belts so that the goat could pull it. The cart's wheels were old bicycle wheels. I had a lot of fun with the goat and cart. He was pretty good at pulling. However, stopping and turning were a bit of a problem. I kept having to get out of the cart to stop or turn him in another direction!

Christmas of 1944 was celebrated differently than usual. We had started going to the Reformed Church in Waardenburg when the firing of the allied artillery made crossing the Waal Bridge to Zaltbommel too risky. But, since our church in Waardenburg was located next to a school building that was used for ammunition storage (a risky proximity for crowds of celebrants with lit candles), the German Commandant arranged for us to march under German guard to another church in Neerynen. I remember going with Pieter and Gellie. The route took us over the dike after curfew, both of which were ordinarily forbidden. The north side of the dike was lined with a whole series of heavy machine guns, part of the ack-ack defense of the Waal bridges. The soldiers who manned the guns laughed and joked as we walked by. Our German guards marched ahead, alongside, and behind us. I walked close to a guard on the right side. His rifle had a bayonett on it. That impressed me! When we got to the church at Neerynen, the guards stayed outside.

Inside the church, there stood a large Christmas tree decorated with live candles. We sang Christmas songs, and Jan Davids told a Christmas story. Then they passed around a basket of currant buns (krentenbolen) – Mmm, what a treat! The march back home was a neat experience under the cool, clear, starry night sky. We again passed the machine guns, still manned by jovial, laughing soldiers.

Neerynen church where we celebrated Christmas in 1944. Modern photo by Sy Byle.

Fall of 1944 through spring of 1945 saw a lot more fighter and dive-bomber activity. I enjoyed watching their kind of cat-and-mouse game as they came in to harass the Germans. The main German anti-aircraft artillery installations were on the west side of the train dike, as was our house. The allied fighters would sometimes fly real low on the east side of the dike, pop over the dike behind the woods, and be upon the artillery before they could react. These fighter planes looked like tanks (P-47). The Germans grew wise to the game and placed two heavy machine guns dug into the dike on the west side, within half a mile of where the fighters had flown over. I watched the gunners working to dig in and thought they would easily blow the fighter planes out of the air! The Germans attempt to surprise the fighters must not have been very successful, as I saw three fighters strafe the devil out of the dug-in machine guns. I thought either the planes had seen the guns in time, or the underground had given the allied fighters information. I kind of felt sorry for the machine-gunners. I had never seen such intense strafing. The planes made very short circles, staying low on the east side of the dike so the main body of the air-defense could not shoot at them. They absolutely hammered the machine-gun nest. As I watched from our house, I expected one or more of the planes to go down, but none did. All three flew north real low and disappeared. The Germans soon abandoned the idea.

A couple of days after that attack, I saw German soldiers in a big funeral procession. They marched, carrying two or three caskets. We had no way of knowing if the dead were from the machine gun installation, but I had an idea that they were. A neighbor suggested the dead must have included "een hooge" (a high-ranking officer), as they usually did not have that large of a procession.

The Germans had stationed a number of fighter planes hidden in the edges of the woods in order to shoot down crippled, allied bombers returning from bombing raids over Germany. Limping behind the main formation, these bombers made an easy target. One occassion stands out in my memory. Six German fighters flew in low, coming from the area of Geldermalsen, and rose steeply up under a crippled B-17. Soon, I saw one fighter spin away smoking – the pilot did not jump. To my surprise, two more fighters went down! The remaining three spread out but kept up the attack. Finally, the old bomber went down. Several allied flyers jumped out. This kind of attack happened almost daily during the last part of the war, though I never again saw three German fighters get shot down by one B-17. Usually, the crippled bombers went down quickly in smoke, sometimes flames.

I always found it entertaining to watch the Germans try to find the downed flyers before the Underground did. I could see them take off with trucks or motorcycles in the direction of the parachutes. The Germans had more success at retrieving flyers during the day. But at night, the Underground had a better chance. Once the allies were stationed in Holland, it became even easier to return them to base.

Throughout the war, the Germans would raid barns, often using dogs, as hay mounds were popular places to hide. If they found allied flyers or Jews, the owners of the barn stood a good chance of being shot on the spot! Our farm was never raided, but we heard about these raids. One day, when walking along a swamp behind our neighbor, Jielis van Driel's place, I heard a voice from the swamp among the reeds and cattails. "Jonge! zyn de Duisers al weg? (Boy! are the Germans gone?)" I answered, "Yes," as I had seen a couple of trucks drive through the Zantweg. The Germans were searching for men to send to work in the factories in Germany – not a popular place to work, as they were the targets of the allied bombers! Men like my dad, who provided food and services necessary to the State, had a permit that exempted him. But a lot of young men hid on the farms, having run from the cities to avoid being hauled away to work.

New Year's Day, 1945 was the biggest event of the war for our family. It had started as a normal day. Heit was prunning the orchard and had grafted a couple of trees. Piet and Gellie hosted about seventeen friends for a skating party. Mem had gone to

P-51

P-47

P-38

B-17

Allied aircraft over Holland, WWII. Sketch by Darryl Byle (© 2014).
Used by permission. These are the planes I got to know well.

Postcard of Neerynen Castle, circa 1950.

Waardenburg. Geertje was sleeping upstairs in the house. I played with my friend Jan van Vliet in front of his house, which was on the other side of the railroad from ours. We heard planes coming, then the German anti-air defense started shooting like crazy. Jan and I dove into the ditch, which had ice in it. The fighting did not last long. It had only been a small formation of English bombers. I do not recall any fighter escorts or dive bombers. But when it was over, I got up and looked back towards our house – the peak of our roof was gone! I ran down the Zantweg under the railroad viaduct, which was, incidentally, loaded with explosives. Once I had run past Hannes Blom's house, I could see the smoking rubble that had been our house. A whole bunch of people were there, milling in and around the smoldering rubble. As I was running towards the ruin, a woman saw me and yelled, "Daar is Auké!" They had been looking for me, as they weren't sure where I was. I ran to my Mom and Dad. Mem put her arms around me. Heit stood nearby, looking dazed, wet and bloody.

Heit had run into the house, upon seeing the planes come, and rescued Geertje out of her crib upstairs. Gellie had run to the house, too, and waited anxiously by the door for Heit and Geertje, before running for the shelter of the woods. They had not run far from the house before three bombs hit – one near the front door, one next to the side of the house, and one on the pond where the party had been skating. The blast threw Gellie and Heit, with Geertje in his arms, to the ground, covered in icy mud and water. A big piece of ice had hit Heit in the ribs. They were able to get up, though, and they ran to the woods behind the house, where Piet and the fifteen friends were laying. Once the fighting stopped, Heit and the others had emerged, returning to find the house demolished and smoldering. How Mem had gotten home so fast is beyond me. I had run home right away from much closer a distance than where Mem was in Waardenburg. Now, as an adult, having thought through the range of possible scenarios, the only way I can figure that she could have beaten me was for her to have ridden her bicycle during the bombing!

Later that day, as we were sorting through the rubble, a German officer came and offered to put up a guard at night, since we would have to quit the place for curfew at eight o'clock. Heit expressed his appreciation, but declined the offer. He did not think anyone would steal anything, as there wasn't anything worth stealing. Our Burgemeister (Mayor), Van Wyck, arrived later to take us to a neat brick house in our neighborhood. He informed the owners, Mr. and Mrs. Hendrik van Driel (cousin to Jielis van Driel mentioned earlier), that they would have to take us in. The van Driels seemed less than enthusiastic about sharing their home with such a large family of children. This was understandable, considering that they were middle-aged with no children of their own. But in war time, that's how things were done – arbitrarily. Mrs. van Driel removed all the furniture out of the front room and gave the room to us in which to set up house. Mem made a circuit of our friends and neighbors to ask for pots, pans, dishes and furniture. We kids helped Mem carry these items to the Van Driel's house. The attic served as our sleeping quarters – one long, low room, but at least it was inside. We would stay there only four-and-a-half months, but it seemed an eternity.

Somehow, in the bombing of our house, our cow-and-calf shed managed to stay intact. So Heit continued to keep calves there. About a week after the bombing, Heit went over to feed the calves, but saw only their remains – the guts and calf heads. Somebody must have come during the night, after curfew, and butchered them. Heit figured he knew who had done it but could not prove it. The shed became home to my little yellow dog, while we lived at the Van Driels. He obediently stayed on our place and did not get into trouble. I would often go there to play with him.

Shortly after moving in with the Van Driels, Mem wrote a public note of thanks in De Zaltbommelshe Courant (retrieved from the online archives and sent to me by my friend Willem v.d. Dungen's daughter, Gijsje v.d. Heyden in 2009) as follows:

"Along this road we witness our heartfelt thanks to all who lived with us through the tragic incident of January 1, 1945. In particular, the family J.H. van Driel who took us into their home with love. – Family S. Byl, Waardenburg. Jan. 1945."

Copy of Mem's letter in Zaltbommel Current
(retrieved from online archives by Gijsje v.d. Heijden in 2009.)

I imagine it must have been hard on Mem to keep four kids in a house where we felt so unwelcome. Mrs. van Driel seemed like a crab to me. She had all her furniture removed so that we could not spoil it. She called me a "steam kettle," as I was always running with a stick in my hands making automobile noises – motorcycle, car, truck, and such. I was forbidden to come in the house unless accompanied by my mother. She told me I could not run in her yard. That made no sense to me at all! Thank goodness, their house was close to the Bloms', our friends, so I could play there. I came to resent the Van Driels, and they became a target for me.

Once while everyone was away except Pieter and me, we decided to sample the apricots espaliered against the south side of the house. They, of course, were forbidden to us, along with so many other things. The next day at the dinner table, Mrs. Van Driel confronted everyone – there were five apricots missing from her precious apricot tree. Well, I'll give credit where credit is due, she could count! Pieter had eaten three, I had eaten two, and we had buried the pits, not counting on her having counted all the apricots! Fast-thinking Pieter came to the rescue. He said that the goat had gotten loose and that he had caught the goat and tied it up again. He suggested that the goat must have done it. Score one for Pieter!

Mrs. Van Driel's favorite pet was a big, black and white tomcat. Pieter and neighbor-friend, Wim Blom, decided they would neuter him. They recruited me to catch the cat. The job was right up my alley – anything to get at Mrs. Van Driel. I have to say, I liked the cat. But my dislike for Mrs. Van Driel outweighed my affection toward the cat. When the coast was clear, I got the cat and brought him behind the shed to Pieter and Wim. Wim put the cat, head-first, into a milk can, and held him by the back legs. Pieter did the dirty work, as he had a lot of experience performing the procedure on animals at the farm. The job was over in a jiffy. The cat was turned loose. He took off immediately into the field and did not return to the house for several days. He just sat in the field looking at the house.

Mrs. Van Driel would pour a dish of milk and stand at the door calling the cat, but to no avail! The cat wouldn't have any of it! I watched with interest, as I wondered if we would be implicated. Wartime survival had taught me the art of keeping my mouth shut. And to my surprise, we were never confronted about the ex-tom.

Pieter found a German uniform on the van Driel's place one day. We supposed that the soldier it belonged to had changed into civilian clothes and deserted. In one of the pockets, Pieter found a diamond ring. He brought the uniform and all of its contents in to Mem, who showed Mrs. Van Driel. Mrs. Van Driel promptly claimed it all with the statement, "It was found on our property, therefore it is ours." We kids resented that, too. One did not argue with "the CrabApple," as I referred to her.

The war intensified, the allies were closing in. Our bridge across the Waal to Zaltbommell had come within artillery range. One could often hear a bang in the distance, followed by a whistle and another, bigger bang! Sometimes, cows in the area's pastures would get hit. We benefitted from that, because it meant meat! Dairymen were otherwise reluctant to butcher productive milk cows. The allied artillery, now stationed about fifteen kilometers East of Waardenburg along the Waal River, were rather sporting about their attack of the bridge. They would take regular, hour-long breaks between shelling in order to allow civilian traffic to use the bridge. Somehow, the German artillery had the bridge covered. Whenever allied planes came in, they would get blown out of the sky. I would watch as allied fighters tried strafing the German anti-air defense, or as dive bombers tried sneaking in – they were never successful.

Hitler's growing desperation showed as he began launching the V1 and V2 rockets, aimed for England. The V1 concerned us most, as they flew low and had a tendency to malfunction. One might come down anywhere and explode. If you heard one start to sputter and pop, you knew it was on its way down – and you just hoped that it did not crash near you or your buildings! We heard a V1 sputter one morning while we were still in bed

49

in the van Driels' attic. We spent some tense moments in the knowledge that the rocket was close by and on its way down! Soon a big flash and an explosion that blew the tiles off of the north side of the roof! It had landed in the woods behind our bombed-out house. A family, named Van Mourik, had recently put up a shack there, with Heit's permission, because the Germans had kicked them out of their house. I recalled how adamant the man had been that no one was going to kick him out of his shack. He had believed that he, his wife and two kids would be set there for the duration of the war. Now, his shack had been blown up! In the explosion, the lady of the house had been badly burned. She survived, although I imagine it was a painful recovery, as the doctor had no medication or pain killers to give her.

The V2 rockets flew much higher. One could see them take off, arching way up into the sky. They never came down near us. We learned that the English would intercept them with fighters and shoot them down with some success. The Underground possessed radios, which were outlawed of course, unless you were a N.S.B. party member. So news spread by word of mouth. You had to be very careful who you told what to!

We had another rude awakening one morning at two-thirty, when we heard somebody kicking at the back door and yelling. Mr. van Driel opened the trap door to the attic and said, "Sybe, you go answer!" That really burned me up, that van Driel as the owner would send my dad to answer his door! Heit answered the door. Four armed German soldiers stood outside, pointing their weapons at him. The soldiers "recruited" Heit, at gun point, to be a horse-and-wagon supply transport. He would haul food to the front line, then haul the wounded to the aid station and hospital. They told him to get dressed and come with them.

As I watched Mem stand up under the strain of Heit's absence, alone with us kids at the Van Driels, I admired the calm strength she possessed. At each meal time she would read a chapter out of the Bible and pray aloud, asking God to protect Heit and bring him home safe. The Lord was very real to Mem, and she encouraged us to talk to God. In all the difficult things going on in her life, even in the very present threat of danger, she could still smile at us kids. We adopted her faith as well. I respected Mem and do not recall intentionally giving her a hard time. I cannot say the same for Mr. and Mrs. Van Driel!

Many years later, when we lived in Michigan on the Markadia farm, Heit related to me some of what had happened to him during that time he was away. At the staging area, where the wagons were loaded, Heit saw lines of new recruits being psyched up to "turn the tide for the Führer and save the Fatherland!" In a couple of days, Heit would see some of the same soldiers on his wagon with their limbs blown off. Heit especially remembered one soldier whose face was partly blown away because of a bullet through his cheeks. When Heit delivered him and the others to the aid station, this soldier did not want to go in. He was afraid the allies would come soon, take them all prisoner, and shoot the wounded. An old sergeant came up to the wagon and ordered the young soldier to go into the hospital. When the hospital was later taken by the Canadians, they did not round up and kill the German wounded. They did, however, single out for close watch the German S.S. in the hospital, who would likely kill their own regular soldiers if they suspected one of being too friendly to the allied doctors and nurses.

The same night that Heit was forced to go to the front, another man in the neighborhood, named Jan, was also "recruited." Jan was a single man who lived with his mother. Of course, the allied planes targeted the supply lines to the front. That meant that Heit, Jan, and the other horse-and-wagon transports were frequently under attack! After a few days of going to the front and being shot at by allied fighters, Jan decided he wasn't interested in an early death. While waiting with the wagon at the staging area, Jan asked a boy to hold his horses so he could go relieve himself. Jan fled and never returned. Later, the commander approached Heit and asked why he did not take off, too. Heit told the commander, "You promised that I could go back to my family in a week. I believed you to be a man of your word." In his mind, Heit also realized that if he tried to escape, the Germans would likely retaliate by harming his family. Jan had no family to risk. Fortunately, the commander was indeed a man of his word. Heit returned home to us unhurt.

In the winter months of 1944-45, starvation was rampant in the cities of Holland. By March of '45, the allied forces had worked out a deal with the German high command in order to fly food drops in for the civilian population. I watched big United States planes fly real low in the sky with their big bomb-bay doors open, headed for the cities to drop loads of food supplies. I remember eating some crackers from one of the food drops. I was not too impressed. I liked our bread better! But some people died from the crackers, because they ate so many and so quickly.

I observed a German soldier as I walked along the dike near the Waardenburg school one day. The soldier was shooting at one of the low-flying planes with his rifle. An officer approached him and ordered him to stop. The soldier got very mad, which scared me because I feared he might take out his frustration on me – the nearest available live target.

An unusual sight I saw often that tweaked my interest was a German woodburner truck. One stopped on the road right where Hans Blom and I were playing one day, so we went over and watched as two soldiers worked on it. The soldiers poured small wooden blocks in the top of the burner. The burner resembled a water tank about twenty inches in diameter and about six feet tall. The burner tank had several hatch covers on the bottom end and one big hatch on the top with a couple of pipes protruding from it. The soldiers spent what seemed like fifteen minutes or more stoking and messing around with the burner. Once they had the burner ready, they still had a hard time starting the engine. I could not figure how that kind of system would be preferred over gas or diesel. But it fascinated me.

Later in life, I learned that the woodburner-powered engines operated on the same principle that results in a "backdraft" fire. A fire was started in the furnace then closed down to allow the burner to fill up with flammable gasses which in turn ran the engine. The burner would take ten to twenty minutes to warm up and build up sufficient gasses. Many skills were required to operate and maintain the engine. A driver managed controls that regulated the air flow, fire box temperature, and so on. Maintenance involved draining water from traps, cleaning or replacing filter material, frequent carburetor adjustments, and so on. Ashes had to be disposed of, which posed a fire hazard. For optimal operation dry hardwood of small, uniform shape and size (only one to two inches square) was needed. Charcoal and coal could also be used, but were much messier and heavier. The vehicles were generally slower and definitely more dangerous than those powered by gas or diesel. The burners had many disadvantages compared to gas or diesel engines but they filled a niche due to the scarcity of fuel oil.

Tensions ran high in the spring of 1945. We heard that in the Achter Hoek region of Gelderland, the Germans had just shot forty-six Dutchmen in retaliation for the murder of four Germans by the Underground. This made a lot of Dutch folks angry at the Underground. They thought, "Why would the Underground so rashly risk Dutch lives when the end of the war seemed so imminent?" One of the Germans' rules of reprisal was to kill ten Dutchmen for every one German soldier killed. More Dutchmen would be killed if the murdered German had been an officer. Hostages for retaliation were usually rounded up near the scene of the crime. So, if the Underground sabotaged a train track near where you lived (we lived near a train track and feared this possibility), there was a good chance of being taken hostage. Many of the Underground were young men sixteen to eighteen years of age, hiding in order to avoid deportation as a work prisoner to Germany. In Heit's opinion, they were not very disciplined and did some stupid things. Heit would say that if those in the Underground wanted to fight, they should put on uniforms and fight in the open. A person could flee, although not without peril, to England and join up with the allies.

Auke and Hans Blom watch German soldiers with woodburner truck.
Sketch by Kayla Byle (© 2014).

In Post-war Holland - 1945

The war ended May 5th, 1945. I went to Waardenburg to see the Germans packing and leaving by the truckload and on bicycles, heading east. It was quite a scene to behold. The Germans traveled in groups, wary of the Dutch Underground which had now come "above ground," and wore blue coveralls with armbands that had the letters N.B.S. (Nederlandse Binnenlandse Strydkrachten). A number of Dutch girls who had dated German soldiers stood around the Germans crying and looking scared. They were not allowed to follow their boyfriends to the prisoner of war camps. They knew they might be shot or hung for dating the enemy, as the Underground were hungry for revenge. Although, in Waardenburg, they were handled fairly humanely – had their hair cut off and were imprisoned along with members of the Nazi Party, then forced to work cleaning up rubble from bombed-out buildings, as well as other community service jobs. The Underground would force the girls to sing rather graphic, self-deprecating songs about their relationships with the enemy as they marched public roads to their work sites. As I walked around Waardenburg that day, I also saw a group of German soldiers carrying their rifles and submachine guns

School picture, 1947. Dressed in soldier uniform tailored for me by Gelland.

at the ready. They patrolled the area where the German trucks were being loaded. I ducked behind the brick fire hall in order to avoid them. There were no allied soldiers or police around to keep order.

Following the war came a period of chaos with no police or civil government. Big criminals stayed in hiding until calm civility returned. The anarchy was exciting to me and my buddies. We would go to the former German artillery looking for things we could salvage. I found a bayonet with a Swastika on it. I also collected lots of dynamite and fuses to set it off. We would blow up flower pots or whatever we thought would be fun, making sure of course, that our folks did not find out. It was a wonder that I did not get hurt. The bigger, older boys got to keep the guns. I wanted a Luger pistol but never got one. This was a dark chapter for me as I had acquired a buddy, named Lenike, who was an outstanding fighter and a trouble-maker. He lived near the artillery. I soon found out how bad he was when he tried to get me to steal candy from the Sannen store! I happened to really like the Sannens – Cris Sannen had brought us strawberry jam and some other provisions after our house got bombed; and I delivered about a gallon of milk to them twice a week. So I told Lenike I was not interested. It is good to look back and see how the Lord led, as I am not so sure what I would have done if Lenike had picked someone's place I did not like.

Our neighbors, the Bloms, had geese that would come after me as I walked on the road past their house. There was no detour that would allow me to avoid the geese, and I could not outrun them. So I developed several defense strategies. A hefty stick served as an effective weapon, as the geese did not like getting "massaged," so-to-speak, along-side of their heads and neck. A thin willow-stick would not do the job! Later, when school resumed, I carried my school bag with me. The empty milk bottle from my lunch inside the cloth bag made an impact, shall we say. I would walk backwards with my lunch sack at the ready. The geese would stretch out their necks threateningly and bite at my legs, making them a perfect target for my lunch bag!

Their bite was not half as bad as the beating of their wings. The Bloms were very understanding about the situation and, when home, would chase the geese away. They apologized for their menacing geese, and held no hard feelings toward me for my treatment of them.

Hans Blom was a year younger than me. We played together a lot. On one adventure we camped out in the woods behind our place. A small pond had formed where the V1 had crashed. Near it, we made a tent from two pieces of canvas, one to lay on and the other we hung over a rope tied between two alder trees. We had a couple of blankets to sleep on and under. After we went to sleep, a thunder and lightning storm came up. It woke Hans up but not me. Hans ran home scared (about one mile). Early in the morning, Mem came to the tent in a panic to see what had happened to me. Mrs. Blom had been over and told her that Hans and Auke had gotten scared during the night and run home. As I had not made it home, Mem was worried I might have gotten lost in the woods or fallen in the water! But I had slept through the whole thing. The only one running home had been Hans!

The Bloms were in the fruit business. At their house they always had a box of seconds – apples, pears, cherries were my favorite. The cherries had bird pecks in them, but they were always deliciously ripe. On Saturdays, Hans and I accompanied Mr. Blom to the market in Geldermalsen. We got to ride on the Bloms' wagon that had rubber tires! We felt very important! Mr. Blom would even let us hold the reins most of the trip. The trip would take all day, so lunch was in order – a sandwich, a bottle of cooked milk, and fruit, of course!

One day, Heit announced that he had located an abandoned German barracks and gotten permission to disassemble it. He would use the materials to build us a new house where the old one had been. Boy! I was in seventh heaven. The first thing I did was to crow to Mrs. Van Driel about how happy I was to be getting out of their house! Mem immediately grabbed me by the arm and insisted that I apologize. I said I was sorry, but added that I really meant it that I was happy about leaving. Mem let it go. I

Sketch of Auké fighting off Blom's geese, by Kayla Byle (© 2010).

suppose she was happier than of any of us to be going home.

On a gorgeously sunny day that May I accompanied Heit to the abandoned barracks. We drove a Friesian wagon pulled by two horses. I was simply ecstatic! The barracks sat camouflaged in the woods. It had been empty for a couple of weeks, and a pair of swallows had built a nest over the door. Heit carefully lifted the nest, as it contained baby birds, and placed it in a nearby bush. The adult swallows flew around frantically, dive-bombing Heit and me until they could get back to their nest, now in the bush. I always admired the gentle way Heit had with all animals.

Within a week, Heit had the barracks up. Pieter had helped by staying at our home site to work on the construction while Heit and I rode back and forth hauling the dismantled barracks. Then Heit, Pieter and I worked together to reconstruct the barracks. Heit was good at fixing things up. I was his eager helper. Mem and Gellie fixed up the inside. Geertje watched from the vantage point of her homemade crib. I can recall vividly the incredible feeling of happiness and relief I felt moving in! I do not recall ever returning to the Van Driels.

I remember watching the German soldiers, under Allied guard, as they blew up the ammunition that had been stored in our school, among other places, in Waardenburg. In a field behind our house, the Germans had to put the cases of ammunition in a hole, then run a detonator line from the hole to another hole from which they would ignite explosives that blew the cases up. This process went on for more than a week. After they were done blowing things up, the allied guards forced the Germans to lock arms and run back and forth over the whole field to ensure that no mines or hazardous debris remained in the field.

School resumed once the building had been cleaned. We attended five half-days a week. Another school shared the building with us, because their building could not be used yet. I found it difficult to get into studying, having been accustomed to a looser structure – playing all day, running from bombs, surviving – during the war. But I still had half-days to venture into the world. My parents soon transferred me to a Christian school in Neerynen.

The baker's dog came after me on the public road as I walked past the shop on my way home from school in Neerynen one day. In a panic, I swung my school bag at the dog, as I was accustomed to defending myself from Bloms', our neighbors', fierce geese. My school bag, containing an empty milk bottle from my lunch, hit the dog right on the head. The blow sent the dog rolling down over the dike. I figured the dog got what it deserved, but I had little time to reflect on the matter. The baker saw what happened and took after me. I ran faster than the fat baker, so he had to resort to flinging his wooden shoe at me. The shoe could have seriously injured if not killed me. But it sailed past me and hit the town water pump instead, shattering the shoe, much to my delight and his dismay. I heard him shout some colorful Gelders slang. I kept running. I avoided going past his store for the next few months.

One of the big attractions for me was the Waal River and the Zaltbommel Bridge. The bridge had been damaged by Canadian artillery, reducing bridge traffic to only one lane. That meant a long line of cars and trucks waiting to cross. I had started collecting cigar bands. I would walk the line of cars looking for people smoking cigars then ask them for the cigar bands. Most of the time, they would give one to me. (How could they refuse such a sweet, loveable, 8-year-old, blond boy!) Often the cigar owner would request a song for it – Geef my een cigaare bantje ik heb er al so veel gespaart (Give me a cigar band, I've saved so many already)! A man with an accordion walked up and down the line, too, playing happy songs for tips. I made friends with him, and this worked to my advantage. Sometimes the accordion player would accompany my singing. Other kids tried to take my cigar bands, so I had to fight them off. Why didn't they go sing for the folks and get their own bands – the Chickens!? At that stage in my life, I did get into a lot of scraps!

For example, there were frequent scraps with city kids that had moved out to live with their country relatives after the war. The country folks had food. Many folks in the cities had starved to death. The city kids had a citified dialect which we mocked. They, in turn, mocked our Gelders dialect. They called us Gelderse Aarbeien Vreeters, meaning Strawberry Glutton. "Vreeters" was a term reserved for animals, and served as reason enough to start a fight. My cousin Piet from Hilversum came to stay with us. He was a couple years older than me and did not possess the heavy city dialect. So I was fortunate to have him fighting on my side.

Gellie had a city friend come to visit. As a sweet, loving, considerate little brother, I felt it my duty to help Gellie's friend get countrified. I quickly went to work in and around our pond and swamp collecting a healthy bunch of frogs. I carried them all in a container and climbed through the window of Gellie's bedroom. I put the frogs under the sheets and blankets of the beds. I was just climbing out when, to my dismay, Gellie and her friend entered the room. The friend freaked out, complete with blood-curdling scream, when she saw the frogs! Gellie angrily set upon the task of throwing the cool, slimy frogs out the window. Mem came up and started catching frogs, too. I magnanimously offered to catch and remove the rest, hoping to avoid or at least lessen my impending punishment. But Gelland refused my help. She cleaned the whole room and changed the beds herself. Older brother Pieter to the rescue – having heard the commotion and come up, he thought the whole thing was funny and took the heat off me by laughing.

Another prank I played, Gellie bailed me out of. One of the small dairy farms in our neighborhood belonged to a reclusive, elderly family of one brother and two sisters. I had asked permission to use their orchard as a shortcut to school (would have saved me a whole kilometer), but Jop, the brother, had refused to let me. That irked me, so I plotted a little payback with my friends. On a Saturday morning two friends and I made our way to the recluse's house. We had planned that I would bang on the front door, while my friend Jan van Vliet banged on the side door. The other friend served as a lookout. However, the old man must have seen us coming, because he jumped out at me from the side of the house and startled the devil out of me. He almost grabbed me, but I took off too fast. I literally ran out of my wooden shoes – not my highest moment – and had to walk the rest of the way home in my stockings. Jop did not try to chase me, just picked up my wooden shoes. Gellie saw me arrive home, scared and embarrassed. She went to Jop immediately and rescued my wooden shoes – what a gutsy sister!

I remember wanting some rubber boots like the shoe-maker's son, whom I went to school with. At that time, leather shoes were very hard to come by, and rubber boots were practically nonexistent as rubber had been in high demand for the war effort. I asked my parents if I could buy a pair with my own money. They told me, "yes," so I went to the shoemaker to order some. He said he could get me a pair for 10 gulden on delivery. Every week for many weeks I went to the shoemaker to pick up my rubber boots. I never got them. I grew to thoroughly dislike the shoemaker, because I felt he had lied to me. I contemplated beating the devil out of his son, whom I considered to be a whimp. But I decided against it, as I still held out hope the boots would someday come in.

Clothing was a scarce commodity, so sewing and knitting were much used skills. Mem was always knitting. Gellie could knit and sew, too. She made a soldier's uniform for me by altering an allied soldier's coat and attaching a Dutch army patch with lion insignia. What a sister! I wore that coat proudly. Mem made socks for folks all around. One of the families she knit and darned socks for were the Dykstras – a family with six kids who lived about four miles from us.

When Mem delivered the socks to Dykstras, about once a week, usually on a Saturday, Geertje and I would go along and play. I felt ill at ease at their house without knowing why. We were often invited to stay for the noon meal, which was the main meal of the day. I did not enjoy eating there, because there was always a nagging battle between the parents and the kids over the food. Usually one or two of the kids would not eat their potatoes and meat. Then Mr. or Mrs. Dystra would say, "Look how well Auké eats," – I hated being put on the spot like that. If the dissidents had not finished their potatoes in time for dessert, Mrs. Dykstra would dump the dessert – usually something called "pap," made of oatmeal cooked in milk with a consistency like soup – on top of the unfinished food. Yuck! The dumped-on person had to stay at the table until his or her plate was clean. Often, a slap alongside the head was employed as motivation.

I appreciated my family and home where the atmosphere was calm and congenial. My parents did not go through dramatics to get us to eat at meals – if we kids did not like what was served, we went without. (The only time I recall not eating was when I had the Mumps!) Meals were a pleasant family time where we could talk and ask questions. We also prayed and read the Bible. Dykstras prayed and read the Bible at meals, too, but it did not seem to have the same effect. That helped me realize that a person's heart, not religious actions, was what made a difference. The only food I recall not liking was sugar made from cooked-down sugar beets. But when so many people around us were starving, I learned to appreciate what we had.

One of the Dykstra girls, Wyke, was my age; her sister, Siepe, was a year older than I. They tried to recruit me to beat up on their mean neighbor-boy, Dickie. Dickie and I got along well. I had already beaten him twice on previous occasions. As World War II taught me, "there is no peace without a victor." That put me in a position to negotiate a peace for the girls, rather than fighting. We became buddies, and Dickie treated the girls better – a win-win situation.

We did not have drinking water at the barracks. So Gellie made use of my goat and cart to haul milk cans full of water. That made me feel sorry for my goat and glad when one of the cart wheels collapsed, so that it could not be used. I traded my goat, thanks to Heit's negotiating for me, for three little lambs. I had to bottle-feed them milk until they learned to eat hay, grass, and ground-up cattle feed. They grew well. We eventually put them in the pasture with the cows. One day, when Heit and I went to the pasture to check on them, we saw our family dog, a large, Rottweiler mix, attacking my sheep! One lamb was ripped up rather badly. Heit swiftly slit its throat to put it out of its misery. This also allowed the blood to drain -- we would use the lamb for meat. I could not watch anymore. I realized, too, that we would have to put the dog down. A dog that killed sheep was likely to attack again. An unwritten law of farmers, an owner must put his own animal down, in such a case, or a neighbor had the right to do it. Heit and I drowned the dog in the nearby sloot. That experience discouraged me. I worried that something like that could happen again. I asked Heit to sell the other two lambs.

Heit got a job working on the construction of a new police academy at the location of a former barrack which now served as a jail for war criminals. The job site was just outside Neerynen, where my school was, so I would ride to work with him on the back of the bicycle, then walk the rest of the way to school. One of the people I met there once a week was an N.S.B (Nazi party) man who was serving one year in jail for betraying our country. He would get a day pass to walk home and see his wife and kids. I remembered during the war that he had strutted around so arrogantly with a uniform and boots. Now, his demeanor was changed. He would kindly ask how I was doing whenever we met. I was struck by the difference.

Heit would leave home at six-thirty in the morning and arrive to work about seven o'clock, a full hour before the other workers arrived. He had to pump water out of the footings which had been dug for concrete the day before – a typical problem in The Netherlands (meaning "Lowlands") as much of the country was below sea level, and water would seep into the footings overnight. This job lasted about five or six weeks. I would arrive at school between seven o'clock and seven-fifteen, much to the principal's annoyance. As other boys arrived, we would play soccer. We had no soccer field, so we played alongside the school. The principal's house sat alongside the school, too, and the ball would inevitably get kicked into his flower beds. When that happened, we would have the littlest kid run and ring the bell to the principal's house to ask if he could please get the ball. After a few incidents we were told not to come to school before 8:00 a.m. So we played by the church instead, right in the middle of the road.

In 1946 things started returning to normal. A person had the freedom to go places without permits. I started going to the open market in Geldermalsen, six kilometers from our house. I had saved up 10 gulden from my several odd jobs – harvesting straw-berries, peeling willow branches, and others – for an apprecia-tion present for Mem. One sunny day, I walked to the market by myself. I felt disappointed when I found nothing in the open market that I wanted to buy. I entered a store across the street and looked around. It had artsy-type things, a lot of paintings, and the like. Then, I spied something just right—a vase. It had pretty buttercup flowers painted onto a cream-colored background. I worried that it would cost more than 10 gulden. But, glory be, it was only 8.66 gulden! My next worry was getting the vase home. I was very concerned that I might break the vase carry-ing it, since I had not brought a cloth shop-ping bag with me. Mem and all the la-dies always brought carrying bags when they went shopping. But I was very care-ful, and the vase and I made it home intact. It was such a surprise for Mem! She set it in a visible place where all could see it. The vase even survived our move to the U.S. and all the years be-

Vase that I bought for Mem in 1946.
Modern photo by Sy Byle.

tween then and now. I still like to look at the pretty vase and enjoy the pleasant memories it evokes of Mem and life in Holland. "Her children rise up and call her blessed," it says in Proverbs Chapter Thirty-One of the virtuous woman.

The Dutch government's policy of Rebuilding (Wederopbouw) started. In the summer of 1946, a crew of five or six workmen from Leerdam, ranging in age from eighteen to forty-five, came to our farm in an army surplus G.M.C. truck. I made friends with the workers – one had a younger brother my age. They helped us rebuild our blown-up house. First they sorted and cleaned the bricks from the rubble. I helped, scraping and brushing the cement from the intact bricks. Some cement came off easily, others, like the corner bricks, took more effort. It surprised me how many of the old bricks were still useable, because at first glance, the pile looked like it should have been hauled away. But when we got done, well over 90% of the bricks were salvaged. I got to go to Leerdam a couple of times, riding in the front of the truck with the driver, while the workers rode in the back. I remember loving the smell – a mixture of diesel, motor oil and leather -- and sound of the truck.

Next the workers used the salvaged bricks and began construction. The rebuilding of our house was exciting for me. I watched and helped as much as they would let me. I watched them mix the cement by hand in a wooden tray. Then they shoveled it into two buckets for the brick-layers. I was also interested in the way they laid out a new reed roof. It was neat how they wove string through the reeds to make the thatch. As they wove, they would hit the base of each three-inch layer with a wooden paddle-like tool to keep the reed ends even. The work went quickly. And soon we moved from the barrack into our tidy, new home, which I helped build! Whenever I smell cement, it reminds me of that newly rebuilt home on the Paralelweg.

I remember Gerrit's birthday on November 22, 1946. Gellie took me and Geertje to the Bloms' house. We saw a motorcycle drive by on its way to our house. I watched as the driver parked the motorcycle by leaning it against the house, then went in. I was told that he was the doctor, and that we would soon have a baby brother or sister. When the doctor left, Gellie took us home. Heit was there and took us into the bedroom with Mem. There was Gerrit, cradled in Mem's left arm. A sense of complete happiness washed over me – no more war, we had our house back, all of us were safe and well, the country was returning to normal, and now we had a healthy new baby brother! My world felt whole and hopeful.

Our Waardenburg house, rebuilt in 1946 with bricks salvaged from the original house.

We had our family picture taken. I proudly wore the soldier uniform that Gellie had sewn for me. Five-year-old Geertje cried yelling, "Ik wil niet! (I don't want to!)," and ran away to the woods, when she saw the photographer setting up the camera. Maybe she thought it looked like a machine gun. She seemed sure it would hurt somehow. Pieter and I offered to go get her. But Mem said, "No, Gelland will go." Gellie ran after Geertje, calmed her down, and brought her back. As evidenced by the photo, she still was not happy about it.

Byl family, 1948. From left to right: Sybé, Gelland, Auké, Geertje,
Baukje holding Gerrit, Pieter.

The American Dream

The day that George W. Welsh arrived at our house, in September of 1948, was exciting and memorable. Mr. Welsh was a wealthy businessman from the United States. All of our family stayed home to help receive him. No school for me that day! His dark blue 1947, four-door Chevrolet pulled up the road and stopped in front of our house. One man, Mr. Welsh, sat in the back, while the driver and another man, the interpreter, sat in the front. He had come to meet with my dad and our family about immigrating to the United States.

For a long time, Heit had wanted his own dairy farm, which was out of the question in postwar Holland. While serving on our local district council as a representative of De Party van de Arbeit (Labor Party), he had talked to the Burgemeister (Mayor) to ask his help in securing a sponsor to the United States. It just so happened that the Burgemeister had recently met George W. Welsh, president of the mayors of the U.S.A., at a meeting. Mr. Welsh had been touring Europe to see how America might better help the war torn countries. Our Burgemeister contacted Mr. Welsh, who responded that his business partner would like a dairyman. So a meeting had been arranged, and the day had now arrived.

Mr. Welsh stepped out of the car and immediately began shaking hands with everybody, including me. I remember the French cuff links on his sleeves, the first I had ever seen. He was very outgoing, and I felt very important shaking hands with this important American. As we were shaking, Heit told George that I was "full of machinery." I then said that I really liked his car! Once the interpreter translated what I had said, George threw back his head and laughed. Then Mem served coffee and cookies. She served the coffee Dutch style, of course, which meant that she had already added the cream and sugar to every cup before serving. We found out later, after our move to the U.S., that George liked his coffee black.

George showed us pictures, which we got to keep, of the Markadia Farm in Rockford, Michigan. His business partner, a lady named Miss Margaret De Groot, whose ancestors were Friesian, owned the farm. She wanted us right away. George announced that he had the paper work all ready, and we could leave next week! We were to find out that Miss De Groot was a bright, self-made wealthy businesswoman. George was eager to do her a favor by securing for her this Friesian dairyman. Nothing like politics in action!

Heit and Mem sat dumbfounded. So soon! (Wait time for a sponsor was usually 1 to 3 years.) After much discussion, it was decided that Pieter and Gellie could leave in a week. Heit agreed that the rest of us would follow in four weeks. He would have to sell the house and livestock. We would pack and say goodbyes. I was so excited, looking at the pictures of the farm. I could not wait to get on that big farm with its trucks, tractors and other machinery!

Pieter and Gellie departed September 17th, 1948 – exactly four years to the day that the anti-personnel fragment struck our door! Mr. Welsh took care of all the travel details – visa, plane tickets, people to meet them and get them to their connections, transportation to the farm, etcetera. He even arranged a little publicity in the Grand Rapids newspaper, the Press, and the Dutch paper, Vrye Volk, about the two teenagers from Holland who were coming to start work on the farm and prepare for their family's arrival. Meanwhile, we had a lot to do in a short time. We travelled to Amsterdam for our physicals and shots. Then we took the train from Geldermalsen to Friesland to say goodbye to our relatives. What a blast to travel by train!

Before leaving for Friesland, I had to give away my small dog. He had gone through all the bombing raids with me, helped me find duck nests, and followed me around as my good buddy. He was such a happy dog, and a good watchdog. He stayed at home, did not chase chickens or livestock. Mem wanted the Dykstras to have him, because she was close friends with Mrs. Dykstra. Heit did not like the idea – every dog of Dykstras had turned mean. But time was short, so when we went to their house to say our goodbyes, I took my dog along. I sat behind their shed, holding him close with my arms around him, like I used to during bombing raids. It was the only time during our farewells and leaving for the U.S. that I cried. I cried uncontrollably. I knew my dog could tell that I was sad, but of course he did not know why! It was one of the most gut-wrenching experiences I had ever gone through. When time came for us to go home, the Dykstras had to tie my dog up, because he tried to follow us. My heart hurt for my dog.

While visiting our relatives in Friesland, I remember feeling very happy. My Bepe (Grandma), Heit's mom, let me take her dog, "Pita," a German Shepherd, for walks. I remember eating rye bread topped with grated cheese, a novel experience. At my other Bepe's, Mem's mom, I found some duck eggs in the tall grass by the sloot (water way) in front of her house. If there were tears shed or any sadness in anyone else, I did not notice. My spirits soared high with eager anticipation of life in the United States.

When we returned to Waardenburg, we finished packing and said more goodbyes to friends and neighbors. Soon the big day of our departure arrived. A black, four-door Ford picked us up to take us to Rotterdam where we would board the ship, the New Amsterdam. Although mostly excited, I felt a little sad about leaving. I knew I would miss the land my friends and my dog. I sat in the front seat with Heit and the driver.

We had driven down the road only a couple miles when Mem said she had to throw-up. So we stopped, and Mem got out to vomit. This scene repeated several times. By the time we arrived in Rotterdam, Mem was very sick. We boarded the New Amsterdam. Mem hit the bed and did not leave the cabin until we landed in the United States seven days later. I learned years later from my sister, Gellie, that Mem had not been so eager to leave Holland as Heit. But Mem would come around to love the United States. In fact, Heit was more eager than she to visit Holland after the passing of Mem's mother in 1960.

Aboard the New Amsterdam. For me the boat trip was one great adventure. Heit had his hands full with five-year-old Geertje and one-year-old Gerrit. That worked to my advantage, and I made the most of every opportunity to roam pretty much on my own. The whole boat was mine to explore!

We travelled tourist class, on the lowest of the ship's three decks. Our deck was cluttered with deck chairs, shuffle board, and ping-pong games. I could look up and see the class above us had, among other things, tennis courts. I spied a back wall and a basket with tennis balls. "Oh, boy," I thought, "here I come tennis balls!" I envisioned a great load of fun kicking those balls against the wall. I made my way up the steps, passed through a gate knowing full well it was against the rules, ran straight for the tennis balls, and proceeded with my planned activity. I began kicking the ball against the wall, and if I happened to miss a rebound, the ball was conveniently stopped by a three-foot, steel mesh screen that stretched up from the ship's rails on both sides. Just when I had really started getting into the game, a white-coated steward grabbed me by my left shoulder and marched me down the steps. We located Heit, and the steward explained to him the error of his son's ways. Once the steward left, Heit and I agreed that the steward's manners were less than impressive toward us of the "tourist class." Luckily, Heit had just met a young school teacher from Amsterdam, Koby Westers, who was on her way to Chicago to visit relatives. She offered to take me under her wings, and what a fun, active lady she was!

Koby and I played shuffle board together. She introduced me to ping-pong. She even did hand stands! She also had a bunch of small balls that she juggled. Of course, she encouraged me to juggle, too. I never got beyond juggling two balls at a time. Koby was my kind of person – friendly, energetic, happy, playful, an all-around great person!

On the fourth day out, the New Amsterdam hit a storm. It fascinated me to feel the boat rise to the crest of a mountainous wave, then to plummet down and see only a wall of sea. People all around got sick and threw up over the rails. One preacher we had met put on a good show. He lost his hat in the wind as he ran for the rail, then lost his false teeth right along with what might have been that morning's breakfast over the side of the boat. As neither Koby nor I were sick, I found the situation rather entertaining. The deck was practically empty, which left the shuffle-board and ping-pong tables completely open for us to play at will. We took advantage of the shuffle board, but playing ping-pong was pointless in the storm.

After playing games, Koby and I decided to go have lunch. For a change, we took the elevator instead of the stairs. We were not alone in the elevator. I remember at least one other lady, because as we started descending, she threw up right in front of me, splattering my shoes and socks with vomit. Well, that did it – the elevator could not stop fast enough! As soon as the doors opened, I bolted right back upstairs to the deck, found the rail and let go! Incidentally, that is the last time in my life that I ever threw up. Afterwards, Koby tried to coax me into going down and at least getting some milk and a sandwich. No way! I refused to go to the dining room. So, sweet Koby went down and got lunch for both of us. She brought the food up on deck – a sandwich and fruit for me. We sat on some deck chairs and enjoyed our lunch, amidst the wind and tumultuous scenery.

That evening, Koby and I made it to the dining room for dinner, taking the stairs, of course! The storm was still raging. The staff had locked the sides up on the tables, so the dishes would not fly off. We sat with Heit, who had Geertje and Gerrit with him. He had taken some food to Mem in the cabin, but she could not hold anything down.

On day seven, land came into view. Koby and I stood at the rail watching the Statue of Liberty grow bigger as we got nearer. It was a beautiful day, sunny and bright, so we could see her really clearly. As we got closer to landing in Hoboken, New Jersey, I began to feel sad, realizing that Koby would soon be leaving us. Then I heard Heit and Mem invite Koby to come visit us at Markadia Farm! Mem had come out from the cabin, still looking sickly.

Koby helped Mem down the gang plank. As soon as we got off the gang plank and onto shore, Mem collapsed. We huddled around her, as people scurried past us. Booths were set up at the end of the gang plank for processing immigration papers. Somehow, Heit managed to take care of the paperwork in the midst of the commotion. A lady from the Traveler's Aid came over. Mem was loaded on to a stretcher and taken away to the hospital. Mem later recounted that one of her nurses was a black lady, a new experience for her! Meanwhile, the Traveler's Aid lady took us on an adventure in the city. She set us up in a hotel, something we had never experienced. The first thing I did was go to the bathroom to wash my face. I held a wash cloth under a faucet, turned the faucet on and got a blast of cold water on my head. That was my first encounter with a shower! I ran out of there, yelling for Heit to shut the water off.

Next, the Traveler's Aid lady took me shopping, as I could communicate okay with her in German. Heit stayed at the hotel with Geertje and Gerrit. I was overwhelmed by all that was for sale in the grocery store! She asked me what we liked in the way of food. I am not sure how much I helped, but it was fun. Our walk took us across the street from the Empire State Building. The lady informed me that it was the "tallest building in the world." She also bought me an ice cream cone and cookies.

When Mem was released from the hospital, we boarded the train to Grand Rapids, Michigan. Again, the train ride excited me. I could not wait to see the Markadia Farm. I enjoyed new sights and sounds – rolling hills transformed into vast flat country, passengers speaking English. Best of all, I could walk around and did not get sick! The ride seemed short. I sat, looking out the window some. But we travelled overnight, so we slept in a sleeper car. In the morning our breakfast was brought to us in our car. We arrived in Grand Rapids before noon.

As we pulled in to the Grand Rapids station, I could see Piet and Gellie on the landing with a wheelchair for Mem. Thank goodness, Mem no longer needed it. Gellie was eager to show Mem the house. Pieter wanted to show off the barns and equipment! As soon as the car stopped at the house, I got out and just ran all over the place.

Looking at the farm photos back in Holland, I had determined I would climb to the top of the silos, thinking the openings in the domes were lookouts. So that is what I did the first chance I had. In no time, I ascended the iron bars on the outside of the silo that served as steps to find an eight-inch-wide board spanning the ten-foot distance from the steps to the opening. I crawled carefully on hands and knees across to look out. As the fear in realization of the over-thirty-foot- drop below overcame me, I did not dare turn around on the board. I was terrified that the board might slip off, sending me plunging down all the way to the bottom. I decided to crawl backwards toward the steps,

Photo of Byle Family published in Grand Rapids Press, 1948.
From left to right: Peter, Baukje, Jill, Gertie, Sybé, Gerrit, Sy (Auké).

dreading with every move that the board would give way. With great relief, I finally touched down on the solid top step. The fear in my brain and the creepy feeling in my gut then seemed to migrate to my legs, which started shaking uncontrollably. I never told anyone about my "Markadia board crawl," as I felt stupid for doing it.

As I took in the sights at our new home, my imagination was stirred by the woods on the farm. Comprised mostly of deciduous trees –Maple and Oak -- they exhibited their full fall color. I loved the smell of the leaves. As I walked around, I imagined how the Indians would have run through there – I half-expected them to emerge from behind the trees at any moment! The folks had invited Koby to come visit us on the Markadia Farm, and soon a letter arrived from the big city of Chicago, Illinois – Koby had written to ask if it was still alright to come. Mem fired off a letter saying she was most welcome. Koby came on a sunny afternoon, driven by one of her cousins in his new, tan 1949 Ford convertible. The car was loaded with people, Koby's cousins, but I had eyes only for Koby – well, and the '49 Ford. Her family drove home that day, but she would stay until her temporary visa required her to leave, about two months. She did not seem to have as much interest in me as she did on the New Amsterdam. Instead her interest seemed taken more by Peter who liked Koby right away. That suited me fine, because she had been my friend first. Koby endeared me to her as the fastest, most restless boy she had ever seen, always walking fast or running. (My steam kettle act again.)

At about this same time, we received a letter from the Dykstras in Holland. They had put my dog down, because he had bitten the postman. I was immediately heartbroken and angered at the news. It had only been about three months since our departure. My dog had never even barked at the postman when I had him. I decided Heit had been right, Dykstras were not good animal people!

Our house on Markadia Farm sat near McCarthy Lake, an area inhabited largely by Irish Catholics. Our Irish neighbors, Jim and Mabel Gahan, reached out to us in many kind ways. They had a large family, too -- three boys and two girls. Mrs. Gahan would eventually become my teacher for seventh and eighth grade.

I remember the Gahans invited me to their home for Christmas Day that year. The abundance of their presents amazed me. In Holland, our tradition had been to get gifts on St. Nicholas Day, December 5th. We would set out our wooden shoes filled with carrots and some hay for St. Nicholas' white horse. His helper, Swarte Piet (Black Pete), carried presents in a big sack over his shoulder and would leave one in the wooden shoes for good children. He would also use that bag to haul naughty children

Mem checking the mail on Markadia farm. Mem was a diligent correspondant.

away to Spain! As I watched the Gahan kids unwrap their gifts, I heard Mrs. Gahan say, to my surprise, "Here's one for you, Sy." Wow! I tore the paper off that hummer in a flash, I was so excited. A model Farmall-H tractor, about twelve inches long, emerged from the wrapping. It had rubber tires! I can still smell them when I think back on that first Christmas in America.

That following summer, the Gahans took me along in their 1947, four-door Buick Deluxe to the Ionia Free Fair – my first Fair. They brought a big tub of ice filled with all kinds of bottles of pop in the trunk! (That was cheaper than buying it at the Fair.) In my ignorance, I had not brought any spending money. But I had a lot of fun exploring. For lunch, Gahans bought hamburgers for all of us. And of course, we had our choice of pop. I chose Nesbits Grape. What a treat! Our only fun drink at home had been Kool Aid.

Margaret De Groot hired Jim Gahan to help Heit get acquainted to the American way of farming. Jim would find out, however, that as easy-going as he was, Heit had his own way of doing things. For one thing, Heit did not work on Sundays, other than the feeding and milking of course. On the Markadia Farm, our day of rest started at four o'clock in the morning. We got up, fed and milked the cows, then fed the calves and hogs. One of my jobs was to run one milk can of milk through the DeLaval separator (this was before pipelines and milking herringbones), then feed the skim milk to the hogs. We saved the cream in a small can. We stored the other cans of whole milk in the milk house. A truck would pick up the milk daily at ten o'clock in the morning. The hogs were smart and fun to feed. We fed the calves by placing nippled buckets of milk (handmilked from cows that had just freshened, whose milk could not be sold) on the gate for them to suckle. The big challenge was to keep them from bumping the buckets off the gate. In the summer, I would lay down in the grass while I waited for the calves to eat, watching the clouds and the birds as they floated by. Margaret would often come down to the barn. On winter weekends, she would even carry the milk to the milking house for me.

One Sunday morning, Jim Gahan came over to the milk barn where Heit and I were just finishing up. I was spreading lime on the floor behind the cows – it kept the flies down helped with sanitation. Jim announced that we would have to start mowing the hay that morning. Heit asked me to tell Jim, "We don't work

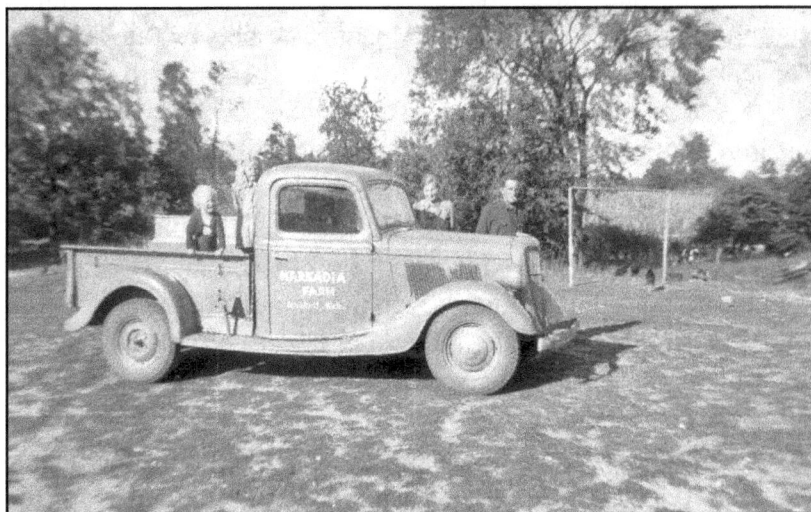

From left to right: Gerrit, Gertie, Baukje, and Sybé on the Markadia Farm, circa 1950.

on Sundays." Man! I hated to tell Jim that, because I figured the American way must be the right way, and Heit's old-fashioned way wrong. I would find out that was not necessarily so.

As it turned out, Heit accomplished his work much more punctually. We harvested our hay and corn before anyone else around. The snow started flying, and Jim still had corn to pick. Ours had long been done and in the corn crib. That experience sold me on the day of rest that God had designed for us – work six days, and the seventh is the Lord's. It sure worked for Heit. And I liked having a day of rest.

At McCarthy Lake, located within the boundaries of Markadia Farm, I kept five pet ducks. I had three white ducks and two mallards. Heit had helped me build a small, tidy duck house at the edge of the lake. The house contained a feeder and employed a sliding closure to protect the ducks from skunks and racoons at night. I had to build a fence enclosure extending into the lake, so I could keep them safe during hunting season. We had trimmed their wings so that they couldn't fly away.

One Sunday morning, when Heit had stayed home to mind a first-calf-heifer, he observed a dastardly deed by a hunter who had been given Margaret's permission to hunt on the property. The hunter had checked in with Heit earlier that morning, stating his intent to hunt rabbits. But once he saw our family's car leave for church (Peter drove), he walked over to the lake, directly to my duck enclosure. Heit watched as the hunter rested his gun on the fence and shot all five ducks! Heit rushed over to confront the man as he was fishing the ducks out of the lake. The hunter jumped, startled to see Heit there. He quickly offered to give Heit the ducks. Heit, disgusted by the man's behavior, replied, "Those don't look like rabbits to me. No, we don't want to eat our son's pets. Take them, and never come back!" I was frustrated and hurt by the news. How could someone just blow all my efforts away in seconds like that!? I never kept ducks again. But I did raise some homing and fancy-tailed pigeons. Several weeks later, Margaret received a phone call from the hunter, appealing to her to let him hunt on her place again. She

Markadia Farm and McCarthy Lake, circa 1950. Aerial photo.

related to Heit that she let him have it with both barrels, so to speak, and told him in no uncertain terms to never set foot on her farm again.

In our district, we had no public school, only a Catholic school, St. Patrick's. As a result, ours was the lowest tax district in the state of Michigan. I entered the nearest public school, Cannonsburg School, about three miles away. Margaret De Groot drove me on my first day in a green, 1948, two-door Dodge. She introduced me to Mrs. Walsh, who taught first through fourth grades in the downstairs portion of the two-story school house. "What is your name, young man?" Mrs. Walsh asked. "Auké Byle," I replied. Mrs. Walsh looked at me blankly for a moment, then instructed me to write my name on the blackboard. After writing my name, "Auké," Mrs. Walsh shook her head and motioned for me to write more. So I wrote my middle name, Siebren. Mrs. Walsh then stepped up and erased everything except for "Si." "Si," she said, "Your name is, Si." What a thrill to hear my new American name! I could hardly wait to tell my folks.

School was mostly fun for me. Mrs. Walsh and I got along great. She was a no nonsense farm lady, and she drove a 1947 light blue, two-door Pontiac Chieftan. The kids played American football, not my game, soccer, but I did okay with that. Baseball was harder – hitting that small ball with a bat was a challenge. I got good at catching. It was easier, and I could practice at home by throwing the ball against the barn and scooping it up. Even though I was eleven years old, I was placed in the first grade. I had to learn to read and write in English – intense work. I did Math with the fourth grade, which was easy for me. By the end of the school year, I had graduated to the fifth grade. I already knew all the big kids, and I knew who could beat me in a fight. I made sure that I made buddies with the three toughest boys – Tom Wheeler, Donny Becket and Jim Becket.

On one beautiful sunny day in April, 1949, I went to the Beckets' house to play. It was April 2nd, my twelfth birthday, and my first American birthday. The Becket place was fun. They had an old barn, a gray horse and a buggy. Donny and Jim's mother had passed away several years before, so their oldest sister, Marylee, in her early twenties, managed the family. That day Donny drove us boys around with the horse and buggy. We rode through the woods and on sandy hillside trails. I felt like we had been transported back into the 1800s and the Wild West Indian times. When we returned to the house, Alice, the baby sister, came out and told us we were supposed to come into the house – that Marylee had something for us. (Alice was a vivacious little curly-haired red-head, who would later become my children's aunt, Alice Shear.) When we got inside, there on the kitchen table sat a chocolate cake, made by Marylee, with twelve candles on it! I had never had a birthday cake before. In Holland, the most we ever had was an almond pastie formed into the shape of the first letter of one's name. The Beckets all sang "Happy Birthday," and urged me to blow out the candles. I felt both embarrassed and delighted.

Learning a new language and culture has its bumps and surprises. I figured I knew English pretty well, and my folks looked to me for guidance. So when I went to my first school picnic in Townsend Park, June, 1949, I had to get myself there, provide the food, etcetera. The school had asked each kid to contribute a dish for the picnic. I was asked to bring potato salad. No one at home could help me figure out what that was. Neither my parents, nor Peter spoke English very well, and they had little knowledge of American cooking. Jill had moved away to nursing school in Cutlerville. So I, the twelve-year-old English expert, decided to bring a bag of potatoes and a jar of salad dressing, figuring that they would peel and cook the potatoes in the club house at the park.

At noon on the day of the picnic, the teachers drove their cars to the park, about a mile from the school, while the students were turned loose to wander to the park on our own, unsupervised. I did not realize the mistake I had made with the raw potatoes until some loudmouths en route to the park laughed at me and told me how stupid I was. Consequently, the potatoes soon found new homes. I threw them, with fair accuracy, at whoever made rude remarks. By the time I arrived at the park, all the potatoes were gone, and I felt vindicated. Mrs. Harrington, the school cook,

Cannonsburg School, circa 1950.

bless her heart, did use my jar of salad dressing.

For entertainment, every Friday afternoon, the whole school watched a movie together upstairs. After watching a movie about World War II one day, Mrs. Dewey, who taught fifth through eighth grades, stood up and bragged that her husband had served as a B17 bombardier. She stated that the bombardiers had pin-point accuracy! Inside, I boiled, the memory of how three years ago B17s had bombed our house still fresh in my mind. I jumped up and yelled, "If they were so accurate, how come they hit our house, miles away from the Germans?!" From that point on, Mrs. Dewey and I were at war.

The next school year, 1949, I started upstairs in Mrs. Dewey's class. I was delighted to be upstairs with kids my own age. However, with our relationship already soured by our disagreement over the B17 bombers, Mrs. Dewey and I seemed constantly on a collision course. For one thing, she drove a 1949 Studebaker – a ridiculous car, in my opinion. One could hardly tell the front end from the back. Also, Mrs. Dewey seemed to play favorites.

One day, Jim Becket and I decided to give a boy named Frank, the scare of his life. Frank, the "teacher's pet," had ratted on one of us when he was monitoring the upstairs classes during lunch. As Frank got on his bicycle, Jim stepped on the left side and I on the right. We lifted the back wheel, grabbed the steering wheel, and then proceeded downhill towards the highway. We threatened to throw him in front of a car or truck. To our delight, Frank started screaming bloody-murder. Just before reaching the highway, we shoved him into the ditch. Of course, by the time we arrived for school the next day, Frank had told Mrs. Dewey all about it. Mrs. Dewey pulled one of her tricks, for which I despised her. She excused Jim, but announced that Si would stay in for recess all week! At lunch I calmly ate my sandwich, then watched as Jim left down the steps. I bolted for the fire escape and climbed down to the playground. Strangely, there were no consequences for my act of defiance. I never did stay in.

Cannonsburg School sat on a nice big hill, great for sledding. The gentler slope on one side led into a field and worked great for the first through fourth graders. The steeper side paralleled the road, which made a faster, more exciting ride for us big kids. One day, as I had just started sledding downhill, the lousy bell rang. Not about to stop, I finished my sled ride all the way down. As a result, I sauntered in to class a couple minutes late. Mrs. Dewey demanded an explanation. I told her that I had to walk up the hill along the road. She replied by informing me that I was not allowed to go down that hill. I countered, that was a surprise to me, since all the other big kids did it. Mrs. Dewey directed me to bring her my sled -- she would "impound" it. I answered back, "No way! Not unless all the other kids have to!" She then told another student, Jack, to retrieve my sled. I raced out and beat Jack to my sled. I picked it up and told him I would bust his head with it. Jack stayed back. Soon, Mrs. Dewey stuck her head out the window to find out why Jack had not returned yet with my sled. Jack whined to her that I was going to hit him with it. He had got that right! Mrs. Dewey yelled for us both to come back up, and that she would inform my dad when he came to pick me up! That did not worry me, since I knew Peter would be picking me up, and I could count on him as my defender.

Sure enough, at four-thirty, Peter came upstairs, and Mrs. Dewey informed him that I would have to stay until five o'clock every evening after school. Peter replied, "No way. Si has to go home with me to milk cows." He turned to me, "Si, get your coat. Let's go." So he stood between Mrs. Dewey and me, and we went home – again with no consequences.

One more incident with Mrs. Dewey featured the same boy, Jack, at center stage. At lunch, a surplus cherry program provided a portion of canned cherries to the school kids. We each brought a dish and a spoon, and placed them on our desk. Our teacher would then come around and fill each student's dish with cherries before heading downstairs to eat lunch with the other teacher, Mrs. Walsh. Mrs. Dewey usually left a student monitor in charge of the class. On one particular occasion, I had just finished my cherries when Jack grabbed my dish and spoon and threw them out the window. I jumped up in hot pursuit, grabbed Jack, and threw him against the wall with my shoulder in his gut. "Get my dish and spoon or I'll throw you out the window," I demanded. "You won't throw me out," he bragged. Well, I went at it whole-heartedly, with the whole upstairs cheering me on. Jack panicked and began kicking and screaming. I had him partly out the window, when Mrs. Dewey stormed in. I heard her yell something. I dropped Jack, and told her that since he had thrown my dish and spoon out the window, I figured I would throw him out the window. For once Mrs. Dewey showed some sense. She said to Jack, who stood whimpering, what a fool he was to throw Sy's dish out, of all people! She had him go fetch my dish. Meanwhile, she proclaimed that I would no doubt wind up in Sing-Sing prison someday. When Jack returned, Mrs. Dewey instructed him to apologize. Ah, victory, sweet victory! I considered Mrs. Dewey's comment about Sing-Sing a compliment. She did not know how Mem was praying for me.

Byle family in front of our house on Markadia Farm, 1950.
From left to right: Peter, Gertie, Sy, Baukje, Jill holding Gerrit, Sybé.

Growing up on Markadia Farm

In the fall and spring, Margaret De Groot would drive me to school on her way to work in Grand Rapids. At that time, she ran the publication, Shopping News. I would arrive early to her house, so that I could listen to her radio, which she let me play with. Margaret's mother, known as "Grandma," always gave me two oatmeal-raisin cookies. Then we would ride to school in Margaret's green 1948 Dodge two-door sedan. She would make conversation -- ask me how I liked school and if I was learning any new sports. During winter, sadly for me, Margaret stayed in town, in one of her houses on Warren Avenue in Grand Rapids. That meant I had to walk the three-plus miles in the worst weather. If there was a snow storm Peter would drive me or pick me up, so that I did not suffer. And, really, I did not mind walking. I enjoyed the countryside.

I do recall one cold, sleeting afternoon, everything was ice. I was covered with ice. Icicles clung to my hat. I was wet from the sleet, and the wind chilled me to the bone. Peter was supposed to pick me up, so I did not dare turn in to one of the houses along the way. I started to worry, though, about freezing to death, so I walked close to the edge of the road. That way, if I collapsed, at least I would not be on the road! A vehicle would not be able to stop, the road was so icy. A lot of tree branches were breaking and flying off in the wind. Very dramatic! It made me feel vulnerable as I walked, not sure that I could make it. I had trudged more than halfway home when Peter finally drove up. He was all apologies, afraid I might have frozen or gotten some frost bite. He had slid off the road into the ditch by Henry Kramer's hill. Then once he got the Jeep out, he had difficulty making it up the hill, because of the ice. That Jeep heater felt so good! I was never so happy to see Pieter and the Jeep!

That Jeep and me had another icy experience one Saturday when I decided to drive it out onto McCarthy Lake. The lake had frozen to around six to eight inches thick, so I figured it would be pretty safe to drive on. I was having a ball, cutting doughnuts and other tricks – slowly, of course, about twenty to twenty-five miles per hour. Everything went just fine until, for some reason, I hit the brakes. Instantly, I got a lesson in the physics of Inertia. The Jeep became a projectile, sliding straight ahead for the reeds. I stepped on the gas, turned the steering wheel, all to no avail. I panicked when I realized that I might go through the ice if I hit those reeds. I braced myself. The Jeep slid into the reeds and jolted to a stop. Thank goodness, the ice stayed solid underneath me. I could not get out of there fast enough! I backed out of the reeds, then drove home across the lake, then up the side of the lake by the creek. I never went on the lake again with the Jeep. But the lesson I learned about driving on ice has stood by me well.

That spring, the Jeep and I learned about being high-centered. Heit had an easy-going philosophy about us kids driving. He had allowed Jill to drive Mem to town without a license to shop and run errands. At age twelve, I drove a lot – on the farm, as well as on the roads to and from other fields for farm purposes. One day, I was driving on my way to feed the young stock out at the Malone place in Parnell, a farm adjacent to the Markadia farm that Margaret had recently acquired. Peter had warned me to watch out so that I did not get high-centered on the road. I only half-listened, figuring that with four-wheel-drive and snow tires, which were still on from the winter, I couldn't be stopped. I turned onto Six-Mile Road, a dirt road which was usually very muddy in the spring. I had only travelled about thirty feet when, lo and behold, the Jeep just stopped, leaving the wheels spinning like crazy, muddy water flying all over. I tried turning the steering wheel, putting it in reverse, everything I could think of, but could get absolutely no traction. Finally, I swallowed my pride and walked back to the barn where Peter greeted me with a huge smile. "High-centered, right?" he said. Then, without any further adieu, he got on the Farmall-H tractor and pulled me out with the chain. After that, I was more careful to straddle the ruts.

Miss De Groot and her niece, Diane De Nio, were two of the main reasons I loved the Markadia farm. Diane visited her aunt, whom she called "Margie," most weekends and every summer. Margaret treated Diane like her own daughter. Since Diane and I were the same age, we had many fun adventures together.

When Diane's friend Donna was not with her, she would invite me to go riding on their two riding horses, Empress and Bingo. Empress and Bingo had all the best-quality riding gear. They were well-mannered and, other than kicking at horse flies, remained calm and self-possessed. After riding, we would properly brush the horses down as Heit had shown us to do. Diane was a stickler for following instructions – no shortcuts! Then we cleaned all the leather works with saddle soap and oiled it with Neats foot oil, as "Margie" had shown us.

Diane loved animals. She was also bright and articulate. She diligently worked on my English, quick to correct my grammar and pronunciation. She would look in my mouth and tell me how to hold my tongue in a way that would help me say an American"R" as opposed to the Dutch "R" sound. One of my first days on the farm, she told me to follow her to the straw pile along the chicken coop where Boots, the dog, kept her litter of puppies. Diane had me practice saying "puppies" over and over. I was eager to learn as I wanted to do it right.

Whenever Diane and I went into "Margie's" house, Margaret almost always offered me a coke. I never got coke at home. One time, Diane's dad, Harold, gave me a piece of watermelon. Everyone watched to see if I would like it. But, I did not know how to eat it, so I just stood and stared at it awhile, not sure what to do. Harold came to the rescue, and showed me watermelon-eating technique.

Not all of our get-togethers ended in a good time, however. In particular, Diane's twelfth birthday party ended abruptly and uncomfortably for me. Of course, lots of Diane's girlfriends attended. I was the only boy that had been invited. I went in eager anticipation of all the good food I expected to eat there! We had just gotten started playing tag, when a girl screamed and asked me to leave. I was dumbfounded. I looked at Diane, and, to my consternation, she said I would have to go! I left, hurt and mystified. When I got home, I told Mem that I had been asked to leave, which worried her that I might have done something wrong. So I went to the barn to help Heit. When "Margie" came down to the barn, as she often did, she shed light on the situation. She laughed and said that one of the girls had panicked when the strap to her training-bra broke. The girls had yelled at me to leave at once, but after the strap had been fixed, they were too embarrassed to tell me to come back.

One of my favorite jobs on the farm allowed me to drive the Farmall-H tractor disking fields to prepare them for planting. The corn field sat next to a pond where I could enjoy watching the redwing blackbirds and white crowned sparrows during my lunch break. I remember one white-crowned sparrow that sat on a fence post, singing his little heart out. As I watched I noticed a snapping turtle crawl out of the pond. I drove the tractor over and stopped beside the turtle. It immediately did its turtle thing and pulled into its shell. A mischievous thought entered my head – time for a little science experiment. I took a wooden-handled screwdriver out of the tool box and tied a wire to it. I stopped the tractor engine and tied the other end of the wire to the sparkplug wire. I restarted the engine, then held the screwdriver in front of

Sy and Gerrit on the Farmall-H tractor, circa 1950.

the turtle. I tapped on his shell a few times. To my delight, the turtle snapped at the screwdriver and held on! He did a jump, then let go and retreated into his shell. I did prove that turtles conduct electricity – a shocking experience for the turtle, no doubt. When I drove away, I made sure I did not hit him with the disk. When I came around again to that part of the pond, he had gone.

Margaret De Groot had purchased the Malone Place in Parnell for cash after the former owner, an alcoholic, had burned down his house in a drunken stupor. The property adjoined Margaret's, and her acquisition of it caused rather a stir in the community. I was interested in all the politics involved and would listen intently, as I ran the surge milkers, to Margie telling Heit about the details. Margaret worked the deal through the local priest. Margaret had always donated generously to church fundraisers. A number of locals were upset that they had not had a chance to bid on the property before it was sold. Once it became Margaret's, Heit, Peter and I went there to clean up the barn, fix the fences, and ready the place for farm use.

The barn on the former Malone place contained a lot of

empty beer bottles, each one worth three or four cents. I rounded them up as we cleaned and hid them in the barn, so that I had a stash for cash to spend at the Parnell store. I would trade two bottles for one ice cream drumstick every time I went over to feed the young stock. Only Peter and Heit knew about my stash, and they left my bottles alone – one of the many things I really appreciated about my brother.

One day, I went to the Parnell store with beer bottles in hand and discovered a part of myself that surprised me. When I walked up the steps and grabbed the door handle, I realized the store was closed. I was so set on having that chocolate-covered drumstick that all at once, I felt the urge to kick the door in and go ahead and get it. Instead, I steeled myself, walked back to the Jeep with my two empty beer bottles and sat down in the driver's seat. I sat there awhile in total disbelief that I could get that angry over a lousy drumstick! I tried to figure myself out. Eventually I decided I was acting kind of like an alcoholic, my drumstick was kind of an addiction. So to punish myself, I refrained from going to the Parnell store for four weeks! It was a very real lesson to me at thirteen years of age about the subtle power of addiction.

The first two years of harvests at the Markadia farm we threshed all the grain. Johnny Oldenkamp came over with his threshing machine and old 10-20 McCormick tractor. Both Johnny and his wife spoke some Dutch and attended Plainfield Christian Reformed Church as we did, so Johnny and Heit became good friends. The Oldenkamp family had five boys and one girl. One of the boys, Bill, was my age. He had been the first boy to ever come play with me after we moved to the farm. We had met that first winter when he had brought his sled over and we had gone sledding together down a hill behind Margaret's house.

On the Markadia Farm, we grew wheat, oats, and rye to use as feed for the livestock. Threshing involved a great deal of work by hand. The hardest part was the shocking. Each person would grab two sheaves, one in each hand, then set them head to head with the sheaves held by a working partner. We would stack about twelve sheaves together in a shock before starting a new one. Wheat was easy to shock. Oats were a little tougher to handle. But the rye had miserable little needle-like stickers on the heads, which pricked and stuck to our sweaty skin – very unpleasant! Shocking the rye was one of the hottest, most undesirable jobs on the farm. Pitching and stacking loose hay came in a close second.

Threshing at Johnny Oldenkamp's place.
From left to right: a friend, Gerrit, Johnny O., Heit (on wagon).

Working with the threshing machine was the part I enjoyed because of the excitement and festive spirit of bringing in the harvest. The crew consisted of Heit, Pete, Jill, myself, and a neighbor who was hired for the job. Johnny O. ran the machine. I loved his old McCormick-Deering 10-20 tractor. His son Bill, my friend, still owns and keeps that tractor in running condition. Heit or I usually drove our Farmall-H tractor, pulling a wagon, with which we brought in the shocks from the field to the threshing machine. We worked hard and fast. Mem would bring us our lunch along with a cold beer.

In the spring of 1951, Peter got drafted, much to Heit's

disgust. He told Peter he would be "nothing but cannon meat ('Kannonen Vlees')" in the Korean War. Heit had witnessed that truth first-hand, over and over, as he had hauled wounded German soldiers from the front in his horse and wagon. I tried to explain to Heit about loyalty to country, but to no avail. Heit hated war to his dying day. Mem, too. She had been raised in a Mennonite family, which would not fight, but would serve as nurses or medics. Pete served as a medic, stationed in Germany during his tour of duty.

New combine, 1951. Sy driving, Heit on ground.

Several great new additions came to the farm as a result of Peter leaving. We acquired a second surge milker to make up for the milking Peter used to do, and a new Minneapolis Moline Combine to use instead of the threshing machine. The combine had a five-foot wide head, which meant that it could cut a five-foot wide swath through the field. No more shocking and bundling! We pulled it behind our Minneapolis Moline Z tractor with hand clutch and power take-off! At fourteen years of age, I was to be responsible for running it, so I read the manual from cover to cover. I loved driving it, got to know that combine from stem to stern. I thought the M.M. insignia was pretty neat! And it was more powerful than our Farmall-H. At the time, none of our neighbors had one. If I could have only done field work, driving tractor all day, and not had to milk cows twice-a-day seven-days-a-week, I probably would have stayed on the farm. The other great addition was the arrival of Koby.

Peter had proposed to Koby during her original visit to Markadia Farm. While he was in Germany, they could visit each other on occasion. She had started her immigration papers, and before Peter came home, Koby arrived on the farm. She milked cows and even helped with field work. She and Geertje shared the "girls' room" upstairs, since Jill lived in Cuttlerville at nursing school. Gerrit and I shared the other upstairs bedroom.

Koby and Sy outside tool shed on Markadia Farm, 1953. Pieter in background

One day, as I was driving the Farmall-H, disking a newly cleared field, I spied some small animals running around in the pile of stumps that had been bulldozed onto the edge of the field. They looked like small dogs, but I could not be sure from such a distance. Besides, I lacked confidence in my knowledge of American wildlife. When Koby came out in the Jeep to deliver my lunch, I drove the tractor over close to the stumps to get a closer look. I stopped the tractor, and the small animals disappeared under the stumps. I sat down on the ground by an opening to the stumps, then put a part of my sandwich in front of me next to the hole. I took my jacket off and got it ready to throw over whatever might come out. Sure enough, a cute black and white puppy (not a skunk, fortunately) came out. I quickly threw my coat over him and dove on top. Tippy, as we called him, was about four or five weeks old and had a white tip on his tail. I caught him on a Saturday. The following Monday, Koby and Heit went out and caught Tippy's mother and the other four puppies. They took them to a local animal shelter (or, dog pound, as we called it back then).

Tippy turned out to be one of the smartest farm dogs I would ever know. He had a natural cow dog instinct and would follow Heit around in the morning to bring in the cows for milking. Heit trained Tippy to fetch the cows by name. Heit would tell him, "Get Walnut," and Tippy would herd Walnut to him. Tippy learned which cows would run at him and which would not. He would sneak up and bite the meaner cows from behind. Tippy cleverly uncurled his tail in order to safely walk under the electric fence that enclosed the field. He was a great friend, always eager to please. He loved to hang around the barn with the cows and with Heit.

Tippy in front of our house on Markadia Farm.

Getting acquainted with the wildlife in the United States presented a fun and interesting challenge in our first years of settling here. In Holland, the only wildlife around had been ducks, pheasents, crows, an assortment of smaller birds, and porcupines. On the Markadia farm, we experienced much greater variety in the local fauna. One of wild animals I soon learned to profit from was the muskrat.

We had an elderly neighbor, Henry Kramer, who rented out row boats for fishing on McCarthy Lake and sold bait and vegetables. Henry had done a lot of hunting and trapping in his younger days, but arthritis now slowed him down. He could no longer go trapping, so he talked me into learning how. He furnished me with all of his traps and the best of his floats, which were the real secret to catching the muskrat. He advised me, freely sharing all his trapping tips learned over the years. As long as the lake was not frozen over, I did a whale of a muskrat harvest. I trapped on Saturdays, setting out six to eight floats with four traps on each. I could usually count on four muskrats for each float. The float consisted of two logs about two-and-a-half feet long crossed by two boards to form a square. The boards stuck out about six inches, so that a trap could be attached to the bottom side. A nail stuck out of each log's top center. That was where I stuck the bait – a juicy, ripe apple. To be legal, the bait was required to be at least twelve inches away from the trap. My first year, I caught over eighty muskrats and sold their pelts for $1.50 to $3.50 each. That was big money for me at my age.

Henry told me that chickens loved to eat muskrat. So, after removing the pelts, I would hang three or four up in the chicken coop at night. Those chickens cleaned the meat off the bone in no time. One morning, Mem came into the barn to confront me about leaving the door to the chicken house open overnight. Something had killed some chickens. I felt sure I had closed the door, but had no way to prove it, and started to doubt myself. The next morning, Mem came into the barn to announce that something had gotten into the chickens again, even though she had made sure the door was securely latched before going to bed that night. Now, we all knew that I had not caused the problem. But we were stumped to understand what had opened the door and killed the chickens.

Heit hatched a plan to solve the mystery of the chicken house door. That same night, we parked our light green, two-door 1942 Plymouth about thirty feet from the chicken coop door. It was freezing cold (about 20 degrees Fahrenheit) outside, so the car was a good idea. Heit sat in the front with the double-barrel twelve gauge, I in the back with the twenty-two rifle. We had wedged a two-by-four board against the door in addition to securing the wooden latch. We had not sat there long, when we saw a string of small animals approaching from McCarthy Lake area. The two in the lead were the biggest, with six smaller versions bringing up the rear. We waited to see what they were and what they would do, if anything. Sure enough, those burglars headed straight for the chicken coop. They were raccoons, if you hadn't guessed yet. To our surprise, they started to remove the two-by-four. That provided signal enough for Heit to blast away – rather loud in the car. I rolled down my window, shot once, then scrambled out of the car.

The two larger raccoons, about mid-dog size, rolled around, screaming in pain. My little dog, named Doggie, came running with Mem following right behind him. Mem was terrified by the sounds of the shots and screaming, thinking that Heit had accidentally shot me! She generally did not trust guns and associated them with war and murder. Doggie and I started after a couple of the smaller coons as they scampered to the pig pen area. We cornered them, and they turned around on their back haunches, clawing and biting at Doggie. I had a hard time aiming as Doggie jumped from one to the other. But I did manage to shoot, in between dashes of Doggie, without hitting him. Doggie was an excellent hunting dog, whereas Tippy was the barn and cow dog. They each had their specialty. Heit and I wiped out the entire coon clan. We also secured the door with a metal latch from then on. After that, we did not have any more problems with raccoons eating our chickens. We got educated on "was beeren" (raccoons).

During a deep, theological Sunday school lesson delivered by Mr. Van Zalens at the Plainfield Christian Reformed Church, I told my friend, Bill Oldenkamp, about my muskrat hunting adventures, bragging about how many I had caught in my traps on McCarthy Lake. The next Saturday, Bill came over to see for himself. I took him with me out on the lake in our new row boat. As we found the dead muskrats in the traps, I would remove them and toss them in a pile in back of the boat where Bill sat. Sometimes I would find a muskrat that had not quite drowned yet, and would have to hit it on the head with a club to finish it off. We had checked four of the floats and collected over twelve muskrats, when Bill jumped up suddenly and almost tipped the row boat over. "Dutch," he yelled, "the rats are still alive!" Apparently, I had not given one rat the proper coup de grâce, and he had started walking around by Bill's feet. I quickly grabbed my club and ensured, this time, that the muskrat received a proper "massage" to the head. For some reason, Bill never asked to go along again.

After going three years to Canonsburg School, our district finally opened a public school, which they called, Talbot School. Our friend, Mrs. Mabel Gahan, was hired as the teacher for the one room school, teaching first through eighth grades. She and I got along great and never had any problems. That showed how much a teacher influenced my behavior. Mrs. Gahan helped foster in me a love of reading. A Book Mobile from the county library came out once a month. The librarian would read a story aloud, and we got to peruse the Book Mobile for two books we could check out until the next month. As soon as we read them, we would turn them in to Mrs. Gahan. Since I always finished mine within the first two weeks, Mrs. Gahan would ask if I wanted more to read. She always had some she had picked for me that I really liked. One that I remember, entitled Orange on Top, told about World War II in Holland.

In Talbot School's eight grades, there were twenty-four students. Gary Anderson, Mary Fox and I were the only eighth-graders. We were a fun group. Mrs. Gahan had partnered all the upper class students to lower class students, in order to listen to their reading or help them with their Math. It made for a congenial setting. But there were not quite enough kids to really play a game of baseball. One time, Gary and I stood the rest of the school (just 4th grade and older played) at a game. That meant that one of us pitched while the other fielded. And when we were up to bat, we had to hit at least a double to get each other home! We won, easily. Gary's parents, Herb and Mary Anderson, encouraged me to read their complete set of Zane Grey novels, which I enjoyed.

Another time playing baseball, standing as first baseman, I got spiked – a nasty gash. Mrs. Gahan directed me to remove my shoe and sock, then she cleaned and bandaged it. The next day, she asked if I had soaked it in Epsom salt. I had not. So she put a kettle of water on a plate, got all the classes working, then tended to my wound again. She set two chairs together, face to face, then told me to sit down across from her. She poured a cupful of Epsom salts in a pan, then poured in the hot water from the kettle. Next I had to put my foot in the hot water. Yikes! It was hotter than anything! I broke out in a sweat. Mrs. Gahan kept dunking my foot and pulling it out. Finally, she put my foot on a towel on her lap to dry, and then bandaged the foot. She repeated this procedure every day until she was satisfied that I was safely on the mend.

Mrs. Gahan put her foot down right from the beginning. One day, Tom Fox decided to take the afternoon off from school. When he did not show up at the one o'clock bell, Mrs. Gahan had me monitor the school while she walked over to the Snyders' to call her husband. Mrs. Gahan was back in short order. Jim Gahan showed up with Tom within the hour. Mrs. Gahan went out to the car, took Tom by the ear and marched him into school to his desk. Tom, nor anyone else, ever tried that again.

Another of my favorite things about that year was music class. Mrs. Gahan could play the piano very well. Several times each week, we would sing out of The Golden Book of Favorite Songs. My all-time favorite song was "Spanish Cavalier," page

123. I requested it so often, I still remember the first verse, "A Spanish cavalier stood in his retreat/And on his guitar played a tune dear/The music so sweet they would oftimes repeat/The blessing of my Country and you dear." Mrs. Gahan also taught us to square dance and two-step. She tried to teach us the Polka, too, but we never quite mastered that.

Toward the end of that school year, Mrs. Gahan visited my parents at our house in order to talk to them about sending me on to high school. But to no avail. Heit, who had gone to work full-time as a dairyman at age twelve having only a fourth-grade education, was dead-set against it. I felt very frustrated that my folks would not let me go to high school. But, as a Christian, I felt it would have been wrong for me to run away. Herb and Mary Anderson had taken me to visit Lowell high school and offered to let me stay with them so that I could go. But I could not bring myself to disobey my parents and leave home.

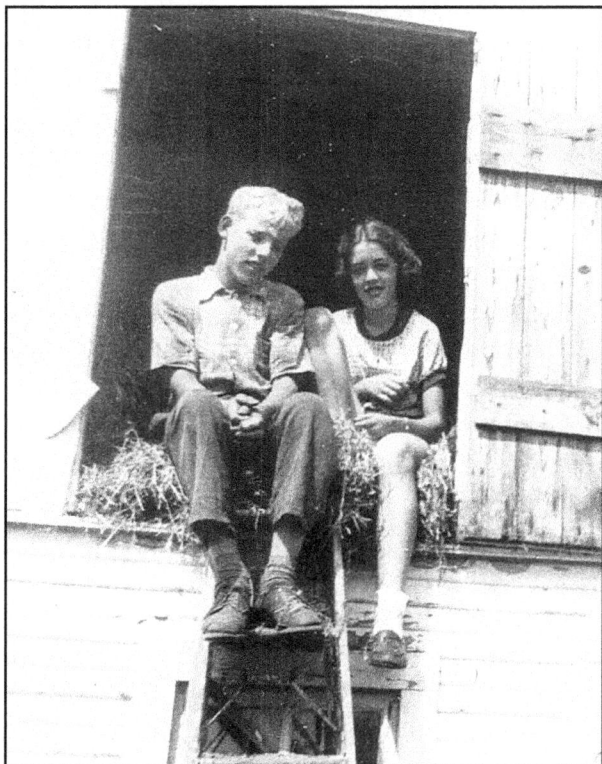

Sy and Diane DeNio, Barn on Markadia Farm.

Margaret De Groot's house on Markadia Farm, circa 1950.

Coming-of-Age

I participated in 4-H from 1949 to 1955, in Dairy, Handicraft and Motor Maintenance. I enjoyed Dairy the most and raised a calf to show at the Fair each year. Margaret's niece, Diane, took Dairy, too, so we did a lot of the work together. However, her calves always beat mine, because she let Heit help her pick them out. I picked my own, and chose mine based on character, rather than body conformation. I knew what the judges were looking for, but I was more interested in having a calf that would be a buddy. Heit had a hard time when my calves became milk cows. I remember one in particular who not only was unafraid of people, but would eat the grain from the other cows' stalls on her way down the milk line to her own. In case you are wondering, cows are very routine-oriented and will go to their assigned stalls on their own.

The Lowell Fair was a big thrill for me. For one thing, the four-day fair meant three glorious nights of no milking! I only ever brought a dairy calf to show, rather than cows, so that I would not have to milk there, and had more free time. I liked to walk to downtown Lowell with my Fair buddies. There, I could eat all-American food! We would eat blueberry pancakes at Show Boat Inn, then be off to Christianson Drug Store for a big fifteen-cent milkshake. Diane always stayed on top of the proper care of our calves. We would bleach their tails, braid them, then comb them out on the day of the show to make them beautifully white and fluffy. We would also paint their horns and hooves with clear nail polish.

I would stay overnight at the fairgrounds in the boys dormitory. An older man slept in the dormitory, too, to supervise. We considered him a grouch. We all slept on army cots which had springs, spaced about every ten inches, for support underneath. On one occasion, three of us boys replaced the springs with strings. We used thin cotton string that would break easily. That night, when "Grouch" plopped himself on the bed, the whole mattress fell through and hit the floor, "Grouch" and all. The timing was perfect, because it was just past "lights out," so "Grouch" had to figure out what had happened in the dark. Apologetically, he finally turned the lights on, against the rules. The lights stayed on while he hooked up all the springs, meanwhile announcing that he would get whoever did this dastardly deed. He never did find us out.

One year, the Fair raffled off a Massey-Harris Pony tractor, and George W. Welsh won it. Since he was out of the country at the time, Margaret accepted it for him and asked if I could drive it home. Heit and I hooked up the cattle trailer behind the Pony tractor, then Bill Oldenkamp and I took turns driving it all the way back to Markadia farm. We had no lights or brakes for the trailer, which was a little risky, even by 1951 standards. With all the hills, we sure could have been rear-ended!

In Handicraft 4-H, Herb and Mary Anderson were our leaders. Their kids, Gary, Karen, Mike and Denny all participated in the club. Herb led the boys and Mary the girls. The girls learned sewing and knitting. We boys accomplished the prescribed woodworking projects – sanding block, bird house, and others – then got to design our own projects. After our work was done we went upstairs for refreshments -- usually cookies, milk and punch -- and games. Socializing with the girls made this a really fun time for us boys. We played games like "Winkum," and our leaders played along, too. Herb and Mary were great at playing games that got all the kids involved.

Sy riding Bea.

Those of us in the Handicraft group would often agree to ride our horses to the meetings, about seven miles for some. We would meet up along the way, and that was the fun of it. Erma Flanagan and I liked to race our horses on the road. Erma was a fun Irish-Catholic girl (she attended St. Patrick's school) and a great horse-rider. The first time we raced, she beat my horse, Bea, and me. I had already ridden over five miles mostly at a gallop. So the next time, I took it a lot easier and beat Erma and her horse. Bea and I beat every time after that. Bea had one character flaw – she hated to slow down and could not stand to have somebody pass her. I had to use a hackamore for her, because she had a tender mouth.

On the days we did not ride, I would drive the Jeep, which was faster and more fun because of its open top. I would pick up Erma and her brother Floyd on the way. At first, Erma's father was concerned about me having a license to drive. I showed him my farm permit, figuring he would not really read it – the permit applied only from sunup to sundown. Erma knew better, but she kept quiet so that she could ride in the Jeep. My bluff worked. I did drive very carefully, as I was afraid of rolling the Jeep over.

One of the woodworking projects I designed myself was a bookcase. I had dismantled a big radio and built it into the center of the bookcase. I won first prize for it locally, earning the right to advance to the State exhibition at the Civic Auditorium in Grand Rapids. We hauled the bookcase down to the auditorium the day before the exhibition would open to the public. When we came back the next day, we could not find my bookcase. We had been looking around the woodworking and handicrafts. Finally, somebody directed us to the electrical department. Sure enough, there among the electric motors, lights, and goods, stood my bookcase with a big, purple First Place ribbon on it – will wonders never cease!

Alvin Potter led the Motor Maintenance 4-H. I learned a lot from him. One thing I still do is to wipe grease zerks off, so that dirt does not get pumped into the bearings. Our group would attend workshops given by the dealerships, in which the dealer's mechanics would provide instruction on motor maintenance topics, and we students would get to practice on vehicles in the shop. The workshop would run for two hours in an evening, with refreshments provided afterward.

One incident that gave Alvin gray hair happened at International Harvester's (manufactured Farmall-H tractors) dealer, Wittenbach Grand in Lowell. This workshop's topic was "valve adjustment." For entertainment, I had brought my boxing gloves. I fought in the Golden Gloves boxing club at the time, sponsored by the Disabled American Veterans. Bill Oldenkamp and I started sparring, just playing around to show off. Most kids thought I was a pretty good boxer, even if I was not. Bill and I did some blocking and counter-punching without really hitting each other. Larry Wittenbach (yes, the dealer's son was in our group) watched for a while and figured he could easily beat me. So he declared he "wanted a piece" of me. He quickly put my light, six-ounce gloves on (Bill had worn them while we were sparring). I replied that I did not want a fight. But Larry rushed at me, wide open. When someone rushes at you, they are at their most vulnerable, and your punch can be most effective. So I decked him with a left hook – consistently my best punch, by far! My heart sank as I watched him fall backward toward the cement sidewalk. He missed the sidewalk by inches, fortunately,

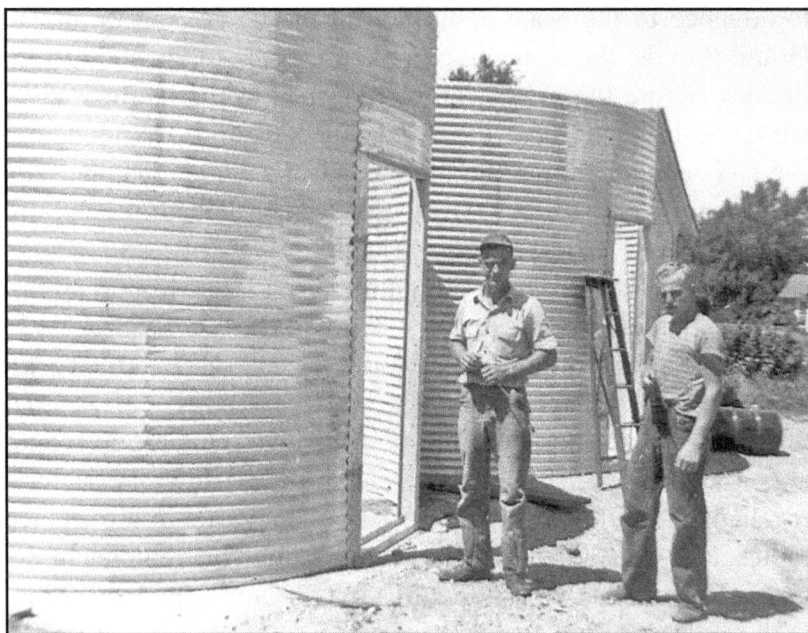

Alvin Potter and Sy, building metal corn cribs, circa 1951.

but still had to be taken to the emergency room. He got forty-plus stitches in his mouth, and some of his teeth would need braces. I remember feeling worried that people would blame me somehow. Our boxing trainer, Wes Ramey (a top-ranking Light Weight - he had beat the World Light Weight Champion, Tony Cansonary, in a non-title bout but could never get a rematch!) had always advised us not to fight anyplace but in the ring. I sure learned he was right! I never took my gloves anywhere again.

Since I had not attended or graduated from high school, I often felt as a young adult that I had been cheated out of an education, like I had a handicap. When I felt challenged by a subject, I would read up on it all that I could, and that helped. Later, serving in the Army, I at first felt inferior to the high school educated boys. But I soon discovered that I could read, comprehend, and write better than most of them. I decided that if I ever had kids, I would encourage them to have as much education as they were willing to work for. Then they would possess the tools to better themselves and do what they wanted to do. In Medical-

Training-Center at Fort Sam Houston, we took a written test every Friday afternoon. I never failed one, as many others did. Those who failed had to attend Marble Head College all day Saturday and Sunday, while those who passed got the weekend off. That provided good incentive to pass. I read and studied our medical textbook, memorizing all the required information. No one else studied that hard that I know of. I realized that I was not necessarily smarter than the others, I just applied myself. I am grateful to the army for giving me confidence in myself. It made a lot of difference in my life. For example, that confidence enabled me to step out and take a chance by leaving a secure job with the state to take on the Head Gardener position for Mr. and Mrs. Edgar F. Kaiser, and later to go into business for myself.

I am thankful, too, for the example Heit and Mem gave me in following God. Their faith convinced me of the reality of God. Over and over, our family witnessed His faithful care of us and the world. As Mem told me when I was three, during that German invasion on May 10th, 1940, Jesus is there beside us throughout our life.

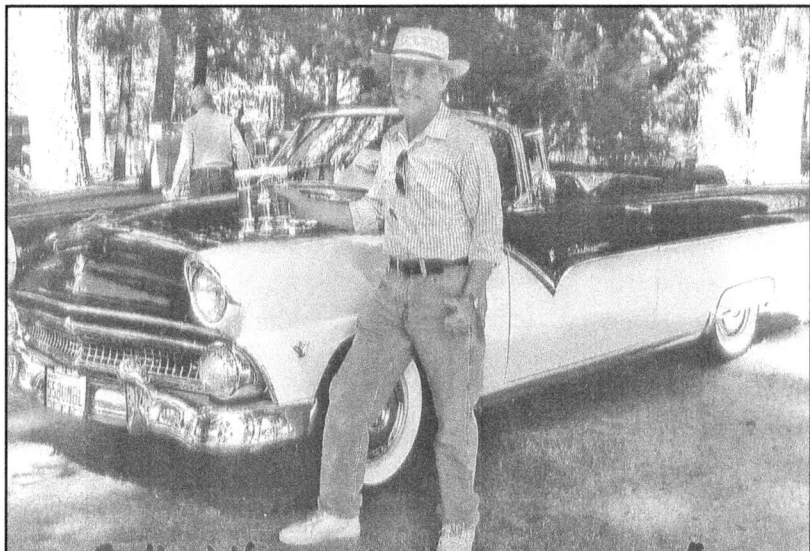

Sy Byle standing with his restored 1955 Ford Sunliner "Bumble bee" and "People's Choice" trophy. Colleville Auto show, 2009. Photo by Ingrid Byle. "I still love cars!" - Sy

Appendices

Appendix A: Margaret De Groot and George W. Welsh
--written by Catherine Byle

Margaret De Groot

Not many can say after a lifetime that they have lived out their dreams. But the woman that sponsored my family from Holland to her farm in the United States in 1948 did. I remember Margaret De Groot as happy, kind, generous, intelligent, and determined.

As a young girl growing up in Grand Rapids, Michigan, Margaret dreamed of being a businesswoman someday. Born on April 1, 1894 to Bert and Ida De Groot, Margaret's family moved several times during her childhood. Her father built houses that the family would live in until the house sold. Margaret had two younger sisters, Clare and Ann. Clare would become mother to Margaret's niece, Diane De Nio, with whom I played during her visits to Margaret's farm.

At age sixteen, Margaret quit high school and entered McLaughlin Business College. She borrowed money from her uncle to pay for school, because her father did not support her decision. That meant she would have to get a job right away to pay the money back. She applied to the college president who found her a job with George W. Welsh. Margaret's first impression of the tall, thin red-head did not fit her expectation of a successful businessman (that is, short, stocky and wearing a grey suit). But together they would become successful business partners and trusted friends.

Welsh's business was printing periodical publications. De Groot started in bookkeeping and stenography. She aimed to learn the business and as Welsh entered politics, she gradually assumed more managerial duties. In 1929, Welsh offered Margaret the partnership. She kept the business solid and growing. Consistently forthright in her business dealings, she did not play the secrecy game. When something smelled fishy, she would let George know.

De Groot began to set her sights on owning an "old house by a lake." In 1934, a co-worker found for her a 102-year-old house on McCarthy Lake. Margaret's father inspected it and found the building to be "as true as the day it was built." Margaret bought the Hannah McCarthy farm, including the house, lake and 120 acres of farmland, for $1,480. She enjoyed country living and would get up early to check on her dairy cows before driving to town to the office at seven in the morning.

Welsh and De Groot sold the business in the mid-1960s. Margaret eventually retired to Florida to escape Welsh's ceaseless business scheming, but would come home to the farm every spring. When Margaret joined her sister Clare De Nio at Heather Hills retirement community in Grand Rapids, her niece Diane, with husband Reg Cridler and family, moved into Margaret's house on the lake.

Margaret De Groot passed away on June 1, 1995 at the age of 101. This small memorial is the least I can do to thank her for who she was and what she did for my family.

George W. Welsh

When my family first met George W. Welsh in our home in Holland in 1948, he was the Mayor of Grand Rapids, Michigan. He had been the Mayor since 1938 and would remain so until 1949. By that time, his business in print media had grown from its small roots as publisher of The Fruit Belt, a publication for fruit growers, to owning several newspapers, such as United Weeklies, the Grand Rapids Chronicle, and the Shopping News.

As a politician, George Welsh championed the needs of the poor and disadvantaged. He had been an orphan himself. He was born in Glasgow, Scotland in 1883. His parents died when George was only eight, shortly after the family immigrated to the United States from Scotland. He attended The Evening Press Newsboys' School, starting as an errand boy and moving up through the ranks to advertising accounts collector. He attended public high school through the eleventh grade and supplemented his education by reading, especially the works of George Handy, a newspaperman who wrote boys' books. He married Shirlie Smith in 1905 and started his own publishing business soon after. When a business student, Margaret DeGroot, proved herself a capable business manager, having started with "The Fruit Belt" as bookkeeper, he readily offered her the partnership, even though she was a woman – a rare feature in printing at that time.

His political life started when he was elected Alderman to Grand Rapids in 1912, representing his children's' school district, the 11th ward. He had a mission to rebuild the old, dilapidated elementary school his daughter attended. That project, as well as construction of a new high school, was completed during his term.

From that seat he went on to serve as a representative in the state House of Representatives, Lieutenant Governor, Grand Rapids City Manager, and Grand Rapids Mayor. According to Margaret De Groot, "once he (Welsh) got an idea that something was good for the city or the state of Michigan, he just never let up." (Quoted from "Margaret De Groot: Pathfinder in the Business World," by Cathie Bloom, Grand Rapids Press, February 5, 1986, p. A13.) During his political career, he initiated and supported many projects and reforms such as work farms for prisoners, rural electrification, and the building of the pipeline to Lake Michigan. As City Manager, he built the Civic Auditorium, now called Welsh Auditorium, in downtown Grand Rapids. As Mayor, he organized the United States Conference of Mayors, which he represented as its president in tours to war-torn Europe, Asia, and Africa in 1947-49.

Welsh is remembered as an honest politician who was great at organizing. He stood for what he believed in the face of staunch opposition, and learned to follow the advice of his mentor, Governor Alex J. Grosbeck, to "hunt the rats," rather than chasing "the mice." Personable and outgoing, he certainly had his enemies. He spoke openly against those politicians who "found that public money is easy to spend and easy to get."

George Welsh passed from this life in 1974 at the age of ninety-one. His wife, Shirlie, preceded him in death in 1970. We will remember him as the wealthy, influential American mayor that made my father's dream of moving to a farm in the U.S. a reality. He served his community, his country, and his world by creating mechanisms that grew success.

Sources

"George Welsh, Longtime Political Figure, Dies at 91," Grand Rapids Press. June 30, 1974.
"George W. Welsh: The stag at evening," Grand Rapids Press. February 22, 1970.
"Margaret De Groot: Pathfinder in the business world," by Cathie Bloom, Grand Rapids Press. February 5, 1986.

Appendix B: Excerpt from Jill's Byl File, written by Jill Haagsma, © 2002. (Used with permission.)

Mr. Welsh was on a "mission," and he was determined that someone would be on the Markadia Farm soon. (I am sure this was Margaret's order or request.) So he said, "What about Pieter and Gelland, could they go right away?" to which dad replied, "Yes, they can leave anytime, if all the paper work is ready." Mr. Welsh took care of everything - visa, plane tickets -- and Pieter and Gelland could be on their way within one week to their new homeland. They boarded a train to Friesland and said a "tearful" goodbye to the beppes, aunts, uncles and cousins. In Gelderland we said good bye to friends and neighbors!

September 17, 1948 we went by car to "schiphol," the airport in Amsterdam. As we came to the counter with our tickets and passports, our picture was taken. We were "celebrities" for a moment. Two teenagers were moving to the U.S.A., to run a dairy farm. The picture appeared in the "Vrye Volk," a newspaper that was read in all the provinces. (I am sure Mr. Welsh had something to do with this. He and Margaret were in the newspaper business.) We boarded the AA to New York. It took 12 hours. In New York, a couple was waiting for us and took us by car to a different airport. There, we were put on a bench in the waiting area and were told to "stay." I don't remember how many hours we waited. We each had our maximum allowance which was 25 dollars, that's all we could take into the US. There was an ice cream stand in the airport. One of us went and got 2 ice cream cones -- hmmm good!!

We had to have our luggage checked before we boarded our next plane. We had 2 suitcases between the two of us. When it was our turn to be checked out the inspector said, "Are you dutch?" to which Peter responded, "Nee, wy zyn niet duitsch, Hitler in the ground," as he said this, he stamped his foot on the ground, he said "Wy zyn Hollanders." "Dutch" sounded like "Deutsch" to us. We did not know that "Dutch" meant "Hollander." We did not like the Germans, and Pieter was very vocal about this. He did not get reprimanded for his foot stamping, they let us go.

Another couple showed up and put us on the next plane. Before we boarded the plane, another picture was taken and appeared in a newspaper -- copies were sent to us. I guess this was another "thing" that George Welsh was responsible for. We flew to Grand Rapids -- our "final destination." September 18, 1948 we arrived safely, where Margaret DeGroot welcomed us and drove us to the Markadia Farm in a "fancy car." There, we were greeted by Mrs. DeGroot, Margaret's widowed mother. Both these ladies spoke "Fries" well. We were finally "Home." We had seen pictures of the farm, now we could "see it" in person. As I think back, how smooth the trip went! We had no traveling experience, did not speak any English. We will be forever grateful to George Welsh who arranged everything so perfectly! Our lives were in the hands of strangers from Amsterdam to Grand Rapids. Today I don't think I would be so trustful!

Our first few weeks were spent with Margaret and her mom, as the farm house was empty and dirty. Margaret had a beautiful big "Mansion," at least in our eyes. Pieter was up early the next morning and explored the farm, etcetera. But before he left the house Mrs. DeGroot fixed him a breakfast he had never before seen -- bacon, eggs, toast and fried potatoes, and orange juice. Our breakfast in Holland consisted of two pieces whole wheat bread, margarine and sugar and a cup of tea. The farmhand came and showed Pieter what the routine of the farm was. He stayed a few days, and then Pieter was on his own. Margaret and her mom stayed on the farm till the snow arrived, then they moved to their home in Grand Rapids. Margaret was quite a farmer herself, she was in the barn daily to help. She went to her office 5 days per week. Gelland cleaned the farm house from top to bottom (there was a picture and a story in the Grand Rapids Press about this). Margaret's sister Ann and her husband owned a furniture store, they furnished our home completely. Margaret's father had died recently and we got his car, a green 1942 Plymouth. October, 1948, dad, mom, Auké, Geertje, and Gerrit crossed the ocean on the New Amsterdam. This took seven days.

www.ingramcontent.com/pod-product-compliance
Lightning Source LLC
Chambersburg PA
CBHW070640030426
42337CB00020B/4097